Simple Foods
for the Pack

Simple Foods for the Pack

BY VIKKI KINMONT & CLAUDIA AXCELL

Illustrated by Bob Kinmont

Sierra Club Books San Francisco 1976

Library of Congress Cataloging in Publication Data

Kinmont, Vikki, 1944–
 Simple foods for the pack.

 Bibliography.
 Includes index.
 1. Outdoor cookery. 2. Backpacking.
I. Axcell, Claudia, 1946– II. Title.
 TX823.K4   641.5'78   75-33271
 ISBN 0-87156-146-8

Design by Jon Goodchild
Production by Charlsen + Johansen & Others
 Manufactured in the United States of America

Third Printing, 1976

This book
is dedicated to
every seeker
along the path.

Tis the gift to be simple
Tis the gift to be free
Tis the gift to come down
Where we ought to be

And when we are in
The place we find just right
We will be in the valley
Of love and delight

When true simplicity
Is gained
To bow and to bend
Will not be a shame

To turn turns
Will be our delight
Till by turning, turning
We come out right

old Shaker song

CONTENTS

FOREWORD

GRANITE AND WILD ONIONS

Menus are for planners, but that high mountain trail life holds its own diversions in store for the traveler who is open to them, plan or not. In the back of this book are two sample menus. To show how they adapt to a real mountain trip, here is what happened on a nine-day walk through the Sierra that I took with Claudia last September.

We started with half a dozen meals already packaged, left over from a trip to the Palisades two weeks before. Then we went to the pantry, and expanded on this nucleus by mixing more cereals and soups, measuring and bagging grains, scrounging the refrigerator for leftovers, and filling a collection of little plastic bottles with herbs and spices. When we were mixing the Spinach Cheese Soup we found plenty of ingredients, so we bagged up four soup rations, even though we were taking only one. The rest would be waiting on the shelf for the next time we suddenly decided to go for a weekend. Claudia baked some journey cakes while I laid out the camping gear. Finally we assembled all our food and cooking gear on the living room floor. The food went into four medium-sized stuff bags: yellow for breakfast, red lunch, blue dinner, and a green one with plastic bottles of olive oil, peanut butter, honey, soy sauce, butter, teas, carob, the herbs and spices, and two whole garlic heads.

By the time we looked up from packing it was late afternoon of the second day of preparations, but we had the trail bug by then. So our friend drove us up to the Pine Creek roadhead and we switchbacked up into the dusk, glad to be afoot and to be getting this steep climb out of the way in the evening cool. After a couple thousand feet we stopped for sweaters and discovered we were hungry. Out came the lunch munchies. We ate nuts and peeled a couple of oranges. Oranges? Well, half a dozen oranges don't weigh *that* much, and they sure are tasty those first days on the trail. We saved the last one a whole week.

> *Hooray for the moon*
> *A day past full*
> *An hour after dark*

Exhaustion fell on us a ways later at a waterless stretch of trail, and we rolled out in the pines to sleep.

Half a mile further in the morning took us to a sunny granite-slab creekbank; no better place for a pot of Mountain Gruel Cereal and lounging over cups of Rose Hip-Mint Tea. No hurry now, hard work all done in the dark. Midafternoon found a graceful curve of creek below Granite Park too tempting so we threw off our packs and swam.

If the oranges surprised you, you'll never believe our first real dinner. Claudia had found an eggplant in the refrigerator; it wouldn't have lasted until we got home, so—waste not want not—she had diced it up with the rest of the leftovers, green peppers, mushrooms, onion and garlic, topped the whole thing with Parmesan cheese and wrapped it in aluminum foil ready to pop out of the pack into the coals. What a timberline treat.

Then it was pancake morning. Out came the new cold-handle 6-inch steel frying pan and in went Buckwheat Pancakes. By the time we were sufficiently stuffed to sit back against a boulder for a morning of reading, there were still half a dozen pancakes left over, enough to bolster the dwindling supply of journey cakes. A baptism of fire on our new frying pan completed the array of kitchen utensils, and they looked nice ranged on a flat rock by the fireplace. Besides the frying pan, which got strapped on the back of the pack with its blackness out of the way, was a 6-cup Mexican enamel pot with matching lid and a bale, along with a paper bag to carry it in; two enamel cups;

two wooden bowls; two teaspoons and a big wooden stirring spoon; a plastic water bottle; a stainless-steel pot scrubber; a pocket knife; and a bandana for lifting hot pots.

This being a day of leisure, we chose long-cooking Plain Brown Rice for dinner and had a cup of vegetable broth garnished with wild onions while we waited for it to boil.

All that loafing made us crave some exercise, so the next morning we ate a quick and early pot of Cold Morning Cereal, washed it down with hot Carob Drink, and went to explore the Royce Lakes, which I had skied across but never seen by summer. While we were picking our way along the talus lakeshore it occurred to us to climb Royce Peak, so we did that, too, with a little more rock climbing than we would have liked, and many snacks of the Mountain Sorrel that grows in the shaded boulder nooks. Finally we found ourselves munching nuts on the summit late in the afternoon, admiring the golden light on the descent and feeling the vibrating quality of the last light over granite slabs before tumbling into camp in full dark and great exhaustion. Just enough energy left to brew two cups of Miso Soup—something wet, warm, and salty before sliding out of consciousness into the night.

Morning found us sleepy, late, and stiff. Slow-fire pancakes—the Brown Rice ones we brought for experiment turned out to be delicious—helped us dally so we didn't even get packed and moving until midafternoon. Those pancake breakfasts were great for slow-moving mornings as well as for restocking the journey cakes for lunch. If we wanted to be quickly up and away, then cereal was definitely the answer. Either way, a little dried fruit left to stew on the evening's last coals was always welcome by dawn. Let's see: put the stewed apricots in one wooden bowl and mix pancakes in the other so we can brew tea in the enamel pot—a good juggler ends up with the lightest pack.

Two days later on the Hilgard Branch of Bear

Creek we ran into my dad and his friend Fletcher about 15 minutes before we expected to. We had been planning this meeting for weeks, and we continued together up toward Selden Pass for a few days of cross-country exploring. Our diets made an interesting contrast. Their food was mainly commercially-packaged dehydrated meals, supplemented with supermarket food and a few freeze-dried treats like Shrimp Cocktail. Years of experience had matched amounts closely to consumption, and after bringing a couple of pounds of lunches back out, they ended up using 1.3 pounds of food each per day. With oranges, eggplant, and younger appetites we carried in 1.4 pounds apiece per day and came out just even, not counting the money we saved by mixing and packaging food for the trail ourselves. But watch those cold seasons. (Just enough food for September in the Sierra can be starvation rations in a blustery April, as I found out that year I was skiing across the Royce Lakes, traversing the crest from Whitney to Yosemite. We had packed the usual summer food, in spite of a friend's warning from his Alaskan experience that we would each need 2½ pounds of food per day, and by the end of three weeks were starving. That cold weather just demands more calories to fight it; more food and especially more fats and oils are needed just to keep on keeping warm.)

Some of the dinners on the menu may look a bit skimpy with soup for the main course, but that doesn't take into account the soups that are thick and rich, the journey cakes that often go along with them, and the occasional bowl of after-dinner popcorn to fill in around the hungry edges. After that, who could ask for more than a pot of tea in the starlight?

Finally it was time to leave over Selden Pass down to the San Joaquin, and face the long climb up Piute Creek that would lead us over the Sierra Crest toward home. Halfway up Piute Creek, in the first welcome shade of forest just past the hottest climbing, we were weaving off the trail culling the last gooseberries when Claudia spotted the strawberries. Tiny red perfect strawberries sequestered under ground-hugging leaves. That did it. Our progress immediately ground down to half a mile an hour as we meandered and crawled our way toward Golden Trout Lake. Never got there that day—didn't get over the crest till the next—but we'd never seen more than the odd green strawberry before and we were delighted, traveling down the afternoon on our bellies.

DOUG ROBINSON
Owens Valley
August 1975

INTRODUCTION

From the earth and the labors of our fellow beings, we take our food. Life preserving life. Life living. It comes to us whole and unprocessed, supplying nourishment for our bodies, minds and spirits, helping us to be strong, clear and alive. When we take away this nourishment, we become weak, dull and diseased. No life. But, there is healing to be found in the purity of nature: food, herbs and quiet times in the mountains and along rivers.

As we wander along mountain paths, seeking the freshness of wild places, cool air, shining light and silence, we need the nourishment of simple foods, in their natural form, as they come to us from the earth. We try to be deserving of it, and to not want more than our needs. Refined and devitalized foods are not part of our needs. Carrying along chocolate bars and prepackaged instant soup breaks the harmony that we seek with nature. Refining food not only takes away the nourishment we need, but also puts unnecessary stress on our already over-burdened environment.

This book is a guide to using whole natural foods while backpacking. It shows you how to carry simple meals that offer nourishment, balance, low cost and good health. The foods are lightweight and long-lasting, and the recipes easily packed and prepared.

We are happy to be able to share these recipes with you and hope that they will be of help, and that you will enjoy expanding on them as you discover new possibilities.

STAPLES

¶ *Bran flakes:* outer coating of the whole wheat berry. Good laxative, high in iron.

¶ *Bulgar or pilaf or ala:* all of these are the same thing—cracked wheat that has been parboiled and dried.

¶ *Carob powder:* or St. John's bread, is the ground pod from the honey locust tree. High in potassium, calcium, and phosphorus. While chocolate takes away from your system, carob adds nutritional value.

¶ *Chia seeds:* the Indians used chia to sustain them on their long marches during migration. Concentrated in protein and food energy, these little seeds may be added to almost anything.

¶ *Date sugar:* ground up dried dates. A good sweetener to begin to get more familiar with.

¶ *Dried fruits:* apricots, peaches, pears, apples, dates, figs, raisins, currants, prunes. Unsulphured, quick, sweet energy.

¶ *Fish:* clams, shrimp, tuna, bonita, anchovies, fish flakes, trout, iriki.

¶ *Flaxseed:* untreated, high in phosphorus and niacin. Its mucilaginous quality aids in digestion and has a laxative effect.

¶ *Fruit juice concentrates:* liquid concentrated juice from fruits and berries found in natural food stores. Somewhat expensive, but a little bit adds a lot of fresh vitamins. A good thing to take along on winter trips.

¶ *Garlic, garlic granules, garlic powder:* fresh garlic is lightweight and easy to carry. Garlic is a good body builder and cleanser. We carry lots of it and use it freely. If it's inconvenient to use fresh garlic, you may substitute ½ teaspoon garlic powder or ¼ teaspoon garlic granules per clove of garlic. Garlic powder is dried ground garlic and garlic granules are garlic juice dried and ground.

¶ *Herbs:* parsley, dill, tarragon, sweet basil, thyme, oregano, chervil, rosemary, bay leaf, cumin, sage, savory.

¶ *Honey:* natural, raw. Honey not only takes the place of sugar, but has added food value. It's easy to carry in a plastic bottle and its weight comes out about the same as refined sugar because of its concentrated sweetness. Generally, substitute half as much honey for sugar.

¶ *Legumes:* lentils, kidneys, pintos, garbanzos, soy, mung, peanuts.

¶ *Milk powder, noninstant:* whole, low-fat, or skim. Good to fortify most foods; adds protein and calcium. Instant: instant powdered milk may be used, but has slightly lower food value.

¶ *Miso:* a salty paste made from fermented soy beans, rice, or wheat; highly concentrated protein.

¶ *Nuts and nut butters:* almonds, pecans, pine nuts, cashews, brazils, filberts and walnuts raw. Another highly concentrated food, rich in protein, calcium, and phosphorus. Use sparingly, a little every day. Almonds and pine nuts are the highest in protein.

¶ *Oils, vegetable, nut, and seed:* unrefined, unhydrogenated. Some recipes call for a specific oil as we feel that it has its own taste and food value. However, you may substitute your favorite or a general mild-flavored one like safflower or corn oil.

¶ *Parmesan cheese:* highest in protein of all cheeses. Also lightweight and easy to carry.

¶ *Polenta:* dried corn that has been ground to an even consistency. Sold in Italian food stores.

¶ *Rose hip powder:* the fruit of the rosebush, dried and ground. High in vitamin C.

¶ *Seaweed:* hijiki, nori, kombu, wakame. Lightweight and very nourishing. Don't take them along and then experiment with your taste. Try them before you go, as their unusual flavor is delightful to some and overwhelming at first to others.

¶ *Seeds and seed butters:* like nuts, seeds are concentrated protein, only easier to digest. High in vitamins and minerals. Use freely.

¶ *Sesame seeds:* unhulled, raw. Higher in calcium than milk. A good source of potassium and phosphorus. An excellent backpacking food as the body needs more of these minerals when exerting energy.

¶ *Soy grits:* cracked soybeans, making a good source of protein; quick-cooking.

¶ *Soy milk powder:* milk powder made from the soybean.

¶ *Tamari soy sauce:* a salty, tasty condiment made from soybeans. Good on grains, noodles, patties, and in soups.

¶ *Vegetable-seasoned broth powder:* makes a balanced potassium broth. May be bought in bulk in most natural food stores.

¶ *Wheat germ flakes:* the untreated embryo of the wheat berry. High in B vitamins.

¶ *Whole grains, whole flours, whole-grain and vegetable noodles:* untreated, unrefined wheat, rice, corn, rye, buckwheat, barley, millet, oats. High in B vitamins, protein.

HINTS

Backpacking, canoeing, climbing—just playing outside puts a lot of stress on our bodies. We need more protein to replace muscle; liquids and salts to replace what we sweat away; fats to help us keep warm; B vitamins to keep nerves and muscles working; and quick-energy foods for fuel. Appetites get bigger, too, so we have allowed for large servings in the recipes. If you are going up high, drinking lots of water will help you to acclimatize faster.

Most of the ingredients used in the recipes may be in your cupboard at home, or they can be easily obtained from natural food and local grocery stores. A note on tuna: Dolphins swim with yellowfin tuna, and are killed right along with them. So we suggest you buy albacore tuna, or bonita.

A simple way to package the meals is to put all the dry ingredients for one recipe in a plastic bag (some recipes require 2 bags), label it, and add liquids in camp. We like to use "zip-lock" type plastic bags since they close airtight, taking up less volume in the pack and keeping the food fresher. Wide-mouth plastic bottles are good for liquids and condiments such as oil, soy sauce, peanut butter and honey, and plastic tubes suitable for packing liquids, butters and pastes are also available. To organize the food in your pack, put all the suppers in one stuff bag, breakfasts in another, and lunches in a third, leaving the condiments in a fourth bag by themselves. For another way of packaging your food, see the section entitled   Grab Bag.

A word on water: may be clear, cold, and running, but still not drinkable. If in doubt, boil the water hard for at least 15 minutes. Signs of pollution are: suds forming in the swirling holes around rocks and along banks; a tone of gray making the creek or lake bottom look muddled; and traces of grazing livestock.

TOOLS

This is a list of the tools we use for cooking on the trail. We feel we need everything on this list, and suggest it as a guideline; however, there are no two packs alike.

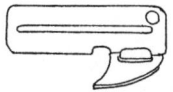

frying pan
large and small cooking pot with lid, stainless or
    enamel
medium-sized bowl, one per person
drinking cup and/or measuring cup
pocketknife, spoon, chopsticks
pancake turner
wooden stir spoon
small strainer
small grater (optional)
small can opener
hot pad
assortment of plastic bottles and containers
plastic bags
pot scrubber
matches
safety pins
biodegradable soap
aluminum foil
grill (optional)
extra piece of rope
camp stove and fuel

1.

Foods to Make at Home

The following foods are to be prepared at home before you go. They are concentrated, and are high energy sources. A little goes a long way. Add them to your usual menu for extra nutrition and fresh homemade flavors, or carry them in your pack for trips when you aren't going to cook and need strength-giving foods.

JOURNEY CAKES

Small cakes, made at home, before the trip. They are high in food value, easy to carry, and long-lasting. Journey cakes are good for lunch or snack, adding a fresh taste to the meal, and they also help round out a meal of cheese or nuts when cooking is impossible.

POLENTA CAKES

Because they contain fresh vegetables, these Polenta Cakes are like small casseroles. They are good accompaniments to soups or fried fish for supper or with cheese for lunch. They always seem to be the first to go out of your pack.

¶ 1 cup polenta or corn meal
¶ 2 tablespoons soy grits
¶ 1 teaspoon salt
¶ 4 cups water
¶ 2 onions, grated or chopped fine
¶ 2 carrots, grated
¶ 2 zucchini, grated or chopped fine
¶ 1 garlic clove, minced
¶ 4 tablespoons sesame butter
¶ ½ cup sunflower seeds
¶ 3 tablespoons tamari soy sauce
¶ 2 teaspoons honey (optional)
¶ 1 tablespoon chia seeds (optional)
¶ ¼ cup milk powder (optional)

Cook polenta and grits in salt and water until very thick, approximately 15 minutes. Meanwhile, sauté vegetables until browned. Combine all ingredients and allow to cool. Form into patties, place on cookie sheet, and bake in slow oven (300°) until firm and golden brown, about 30 to 45 minutes.

VARIATIONS: use nut butters in place of sesame butter; use leftover vegetables (mash before adding); use nuts or pumpkin seeds in place of sunflower seeds; season with herbs such as basil, oregano, savory, chervil, or tarragon.

SEED CAKES

¶ 1 dozen

A different-tasting cake, good with peanut butter and honey, cheese, hot mustard, any sauce or gravy or just plain.

¶ ½ cup polenta or corn meal
¶ 2 tablespoons soy grits
¶ 2 cups water
¶ 1 cup sunflower seeds
¶ ½ cup pumpkin seeds
¶ 2 tablespoons sesame seeds
¶ 2 tablespoons chia seeds
¶ ½ teaspoon salt
¶ 1 teaspoon honey

Combine water, polenta, and soy grits in a saucepan and bring to a boil. Reduce heat and cook slowly until thick enough to hold a mound, stirring occasionally. Meanwhile, grind all seeds except the chia seeds and a few sunflower seeds. When the polenta mixture is done and cooled enough to handle, add seeds, salt, and honey. Mix well with hands and form into patties approximately 2½ inches in diameter. Bake on a cookie sheet at 300° for 30 minutes.

POTATO CAKES

Fresh potato flavor, good with hot mustard.

- ¶ 6 large raw potatoes, with peels, grated
- ¶ 2 carrots, grated
- ¶ 2 onions, chopped
- ¶ 1 garlic clove, minced
- ¶ 2 eggs, beaten
- ¶ 3 tablespoons melted butter
- ¶ 2 teaspoons salt
- ¶ pinch cayenne
- ¶ ¼ to ½ cup whole wheat bread crumbs

Chop and grate vegetables in one bowl and drain. Stir in remaining ingredients; mix with hands. Spread in 8-inch square pan. Bake at 350° for 1 hour. Cut into squares; cool. Wrap individually in wax paper.

SOYBEAN CAKES

¶ 1 dozen

These are especially good with a mild cheese such as Jack or Swiss.

¶   1 cup dry soybeans, soaked overnight and
        cooked
¶   1 onion, chopped fine
¶   1 garlic clove, minced
¶   1 tablespoon fresh parsley, minced
¶   1 tablespoon olive oil
¶   1 tablespoon miso
¶   1 teaspoon tamari soy sauce

Mash beans well in a suribachi (a ceramic bowl with serrated lines on the inside surface, sometimes found in Japanese or natural food stores) or put through a food grinder or ricer. Add remaining ingredients and mix well. The mash should be very thick and hold well when shaped into a ball. Form into patties and bake on a cookie sheet in slow oven (300°) for about 30 minutes. Turn once while baking. Cakes are done when they feel solid. They will be crusty on the outside and soft inside.

VARIATIONS: add leftover cooked grains; carrots are a good addition; season with oregano; pour hot chili sauce over the cakes.

LENTIL RICE CAKES

¶ 1 dozen

These cakes are good with peanut butter, cheese, sauces, soups, or plain.

¶ ⅔ cup brown rice
¶ ⅓ cup lentils
¶ 3 cups water
¶ 1 teaspoon salt
¶ 1 small onion, chopped fine
¶ 1 small carrot, grated
¶ 1 garlic clove, minced
¶ 1 tablespoon parsley, minced
¶ 1 tablespoon olive oil
¶ 1 teaspoon tamari soy sauce

Season with *one* of the following:
¶ 1 teaspoon cumin, ground
¶ ½ teaspoon rosemary, ground
¶ ⅛ teaspoon cloves, ground

Cook the rice and lentils in water with salt, for about 45 minutes (all water should be absorbed), and allow to cool. Mash well with hands, then add rest of ingredients and mix well. Form into patties, place on cookie sheet, and bake at 300° for 30 to 45 minutes. Turn once to allow underside to cook.

BROWN RICE CAKES

¶ 1 dozen

Good for lunch with cheddar cheese or Port Salut. These cakes can also be made in camp.

¶ 1 cup brown rice
¶ 3 cups water
¶ 1 teaspoon salt
¶ 1 carrot, grated
¶ 1 onion, chopped fine
¶ ½ to 1 cup greens, chopped (spinach, mustard greens, sorrel, watercress)
¶ 1 tablespoon olive oil
¶ 1 teaspoon ground ginger

Cook rice in water with salt and allow to cool. Mash well with hands, then add rest of ingredients and continue to mix and mash with hands. If too moist, add a little soy flour. Form into patties and bake on a cookie sheet for 30 to 45 minutes at 300°, turning once. If making these in camp, use wild onions and greens. Form into patties and fry in a little oil. These cakes are good with fish. Sprinkle soy sauce or spread mustard on top if desired.

SPICY WINTER SQUASH CAKES

¶ approximately 1 dozen

Crispy on the outside, soft on the inside. A good winter food with spice to warm you up.

¶ 1 to 1½ cups cooked winter squash
¶ ½ cup dry garbanzo beans, soaked overnight and cooked
¶ ½ cup corn flour or whole wheat flour
¶ 1½ teaspoons cumin, ground
¶ 1½ teaspoons parsley flakes
¶ ½ teaspoon salt
¶ ½ teaspoon garlic granules
¶ ¼ teaspoon cayenne
¶ 1 teaspoon olive oil

Mix all ingredients well and form into patties (about ½ inch thick and 2½ inches across) on cookie sheet. Bake at 375° for 30 to 40 minutes. Good with cheese or cold Peanut Butter Gravy.

I picked my way
Through a mountain road,
And I was greeted
By a smiling violet.

Bashō

BREADS

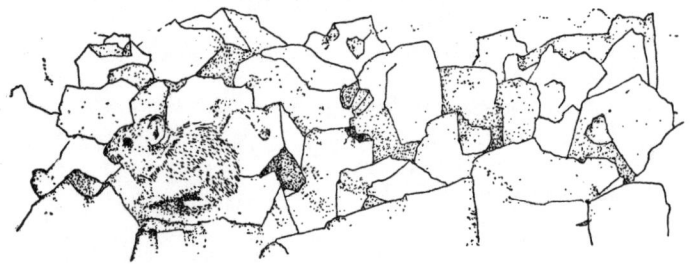

There are so many wonderful
bread recipes around that we
didn't feel it necessary to include
very many. But here are a few we
thought were special. They are
high in protein, one is made with
leftovers, and all can be used to
accompany any meal or eaten
at any time.

ZWIEBACK

This is a good idea for any whole-grain yeasted bread. It makes the bread lightweight and long-lasting. It may be broken into soups or salads for crunchiness.

Slice bread ½ inch thick or a little thicker and bake on open oven racks at 225° for approximately 2½ hours. Carry in a plastic bag.

SESAME CHIA CRACKERS

¶ approximately 24 crackers

Crunchy crackers, easy to make, good with anything on them.

¶   2   cups whole wheat flour *or* 1½ cups oat flour and ¾ cup soy flour
¶   ½ cup sesame seeds
¶   2   tablespoons chia seeds
¶   1   teaspoon salt
¶   ⅓ cup sesame oil
¶   ½ cup water

Put flour, sesame and chia seeds, and salt in a bowl. Stir; add oil and mix in with fork. When all is an even texture, add water and shape into large ball. Roll out between wax paper on which you have sprinkled extra sesame seeds. Cut into cracker shapes. Remove from wax paper, place on ungreased cookie sheet and bake at 375° for 15 to 20 minutes.

HIGH PROTEIN CRACKERS

¶ 2 dozen

Serve for lunch or supper. They take the place of bread and are tasty and crunchy.

¶ 1 cup whole wheat flour
¶ 1 cup rye flour
¶ ½ cup soy flour
¶ ½ cup wheat germ flakes
¶ ½ cup sesame seeds
¶ 1 tablespoon chia seeds
¶ 1 teaspoon coarse-ground sea salt
¶ ⅓ cup corn germ oil
¶ enough cold water to make a stiff dough

Combine dry ingredients, except salt, and mix well. Stir in oil and add water to make stiff dough. Knead a little and let stand a few minutes. Roll out dough very thin, sprinkle on salt and a few extra sesame seeds and roll again, pushing salt and seeds well into dough. Poke with fork, cut into desired shapes. Bake on ungreased cookie sheet at 300° until golden brown and crisp, about 15 to 20 minutes.

CHAPATIS

¶ approximately 1 dozen

These can be made at home and reheated in camp or made right in camp, by patting out between the hands or rolling out on a clean, flat rock with a plastic bottle. They go well with curry and stews or as crackers for lunch. For variety, mix in leftover grains, vegetables or stewed fruits.

¶ 1 cup whole-grain flour (corn, wheat, rye, buckwheat, rice, barley, oat, or any combination)
¶ ½ teaspoon oil
¶ ½ teaspoon salt
¶ ⅓ cup water (approximately)

Combine ingredients, adding enough water to make a stiff dough. Knead until elastic. Form into 1-inch balls and roll out into thin cakes. Roast cakes on both sides on a hot dry pan until they puff.

SESAME SEED BREAD

¶ 1 loaf

Easy to make, a good companion to soups. Slice thin, as a little goes a long way. The sweet, nutty flavor of sesame comes out very well when toasted.

¶ 4 cups whole wheat flour
¶ 1½ cups sesame seeds
¶ 1½ cups wheat germ flakes
¶ 1 cup brown rice flour
¶ 1 cup millet flour
¶ 1 tablespoon oil
¶ 1½ teaspoons salt
¶ 3 cups water

Toast sesame seeds and wheat germ separately in ungreased fry pan, then put in one bowl. Add flours and salt and stir well. Make a well in the center and add oil and water. Stir well. Spoon into well-greased bread pan. Bake at 325° for 1¼ hours or until bread is golden brown and feels firm. Remove from pan right away and cool on rack. For soft crust, brush top with a little oil while still hot.

HIGH PROTEIN LEFTOVERS BREAD

¶ 2 loaves

This is a heavy, tasty bread that keeps well and, when sliced thin, is excellent with soups or spreads.

¶ 5 cups whole wheat flour *or* 4 cups whole wheat and 1 cup rye flour
¶ 1 cup soy flour
¶ 4 cups leftover cooked vegetables and grains, mashed or strained, or, if you have no leftovers, 3 cups cooked millet and 1 cup cooked carrots or other vegetables on hand, mashed or strained
¶ ¼ cup oil
¶ 2 teaspoons salt
¶ vegetable stock or water
¶ corn meal

Mix all ingredients completely, adding a little whole wheat flour if too sticky or a little vegetable stock if too dry. Knead until it is a very even consistency and a bit springy. Divide in half and shape into loaves. Put into two oiled pans that have been sprinkled with coarse corn meal and make a slit about ¼ inch deep in top of each loaf. Moisten the top with water, cover, and let sit in a warm spot 6 to 12 hours, depending on how long you can wait. Bake at 350° for 1 hour.

DRIED FRUIT BREAD

A heavy, sweet bread, high in protein. Good for snacks with peanut butter and Dried Fruit Jam (see page 179) or toasted for breakfast with honey.

¶   3   cups rolled oats
¶   1   cup chopped dried apricots (may be cut with scissors)
¶   3   cups water
¶   1   cup raisins
¶   1   cup dates, pitted and chopped
¶   1   cup mixed nuts, chopped
¶   ¼ cup honey
¶   ¼ cup oil
¶   1   teaspoon anise seed (optional)
¶   ½ teaspoon salt
¶   4   to 4¼ cups whole wheat flour
¶   1   cup millet flour
¶   ½ cup rye flour
¶   ½ cup soy flour
¶   ¼ cup milk powder

In a large bowl, soak oatmeal and apricots in water for 15 minutes. After soaking, add raisins, dates, nuts, honey, oil, anise, and salt. Stir well. Slowly add mixed flours and milk powder and mix well with hands. Turn out on floured board and knead about 150 times. Form into three small loaves, place on flat cookie sheet, and put aside for 10 minutes. Slit tops of loaves, brush lightly with oil, and bake at 375° for 1½ hours. Cool well before packing.

FRUITCAKE

¶ 2 loaves

Excellent luxury snack for winter escapades.
Slice thin, wrap individually. Goes a long way.

¶ 4½ cups whole wheat flour
¶ 1 pound butter
¶ 2 cups honey
¶ 1 tablespoon cinnamon
¶ 1 tablespoon cloves
¶ 1 tablespoon nutmeg
¶ 1 tablespoon allspice
¶ 2 teaspoons mace
¶ 1 teaspoon ginger
¶ 1 teaspoon salt
¶ ½ cup brandy or apple, orange, prune, or
     grape juice
¶ 2 pounds currants
¶ 2 pounds dates
¶ 1½ pounds nuts
¶ ½ pound raisins

Cream butter and honey. Add spices and salt and
stir well. Add flour alternately with ¼ cup
brandy or fruit juice. Fold in dried fruits and
nuts. Line bottoms of 2 oiled loaf pans with a
brown paper sack cut into right shape. Oil again
and pour in cake batter. Place a shallow pan of
water on bottom shelf in oven. Place loaf pans on
upper shelf and bake at 250° for 3 to 3½ hours or
until done. Remove, cool completely. Wrap loaves
in a cheesecloth that has been dipped in brandy
or juice, pour ¼ cup brandy or juice over the top
and wrap airtight in foil. You may make this
months before you eat it or only a week ahead of
time. You might like to add ¼ cup brandy every
couple of weeks or so, or even fruit juice. Just
carefully open the foil, pour liquid over the top,
and reseal.

POCKET FOODS

These are the foods that we like to keep within easy reach, for nourishment at any time. On the trail, for lunch, on a ski tour, in the tent at night or in the rain, floating down the river, sitting on a ledge, or up in a tree. They provide condensed protein energy. And don't forget, just plain dried fruit and nuts make good pocket foods.

HOME-DRIED APPLES

Gravensteins, Pippins or Delicious make the best dried apples, but any kind will do.

Wash apples well. If they have been waxed, use castile soap. Remove core, but leave unpeeled apples whole. Slice in rings ⅛ inch to ¼ inch thick. Hang slices to dry on a string that goes through the center of each of the slices, being sure they don't touch each other. Allow to hang for several days.

TRAIL CRUMBS

Mixtures of dried fruits, nuts, and seeds for munching any time. These are our favorite combinations, but don't feel limited.

almonds, brazils, raisins, soy nuts, dates, carob chips

sunflower seeds and raisins

cashews, raisins, raw peanuts, sunflower seeds, rose hips

almonds and apricots

salted soy nuts and raisins

walnuts, dates, coconut chunks, sunflower seeds, carob chips

pecans and currants

pumpkin seeds and figs

pine nuts

FRUIT LEATHER

A dried fruit sweet treat. Break off pieces to suck on along the trail; it melts in your mouth, a good replacement for hard candy. When you have an excess of fresh ripe fruit or berries, plan ahead and dry some in thin shallow "peels" in the sun. It happens quickly and easily.

¶ apricots
¶ peaches
¶ plums
¶ all berries
¶ apple or pear sauce that has been put through a ricer

Wash and dry ripe fruit as best you can. Place whole fruit in ricer, and mash through into a bowl, leaving just the dry peels or seeds in the ricer. You might like to add almond extract, honey, or lemon juice, depending on taste of fruit. Pour fruit sauce in a puddle in the middle of a glass cake or pie pan and spread to within ½ inch of all edges. It should be the consistency of apple butter. Place in the sun for the day, bringing it in as the sun goes down in order to avoid dew. Cover for the evening with an open paper bag or cheesecloth to keep fruit clean. Return to the sun the following day and repeat until dry. If a storm comes up for the day, put pan in oven at the lowest heat possible and leave the door slightly open. Watch carefully. When fruit is dry enough to be lifted off pan, just continue drying on oven racks so both sides dry. In summertime, it should take 3 to 4 days. When finished, peel off and lay fruit leather on a piece of wax paper and roll up. Place in a plastic bag and store in a cool, dry, dark place.

TOASTED SOYBEANS

¶ approximately 1¼ cups

A crunchy snack, high in protein.

¶ 1 cup soybeans
¶ 4 cups water

Soak soybeans overnight in water. In the morning, strain and reserve the liquid for breads, soups, and so forth. Place drained beans in shallow baking pans and bake, stirring frequently, at 300° for 75 to 90 minutes or until golden in color and crunchy. When done, and still hot, sprinkle soy sauce over the beans and stir until the sauce coats them and dries up. Cool before storing. A good idea is to grind some up, somewhat coarsely, and save them to sprinkle over soups, stews, or salads.

VARIATION: Soak in salted water (1 teaspoon salt to one quart water) and omit soy sauce.

SPICY SEED SNACK

¶ approximately 2¼ cups

These quantities may be varied according to taste.

¶ 1 cup pumpkin seeds
¶ 1 cup sunflower seeds
¶ ¼ cup sesame seeds
¶ 1 tablespoon sesame oil
¶ 1 tablespoon tamari soy sauce
¶ ½ teaspoon cayenne
¶ ½ teaspoon celery seed
¶ ⅛ teaspoon garlic granules (optional)

Mix all ingredients together well in bowl.
Sprinkle into shallow baking pan. Bake at 350° for 25 minutes or so, stirring a couple of times. Store airtight when cool.

FRUIT PEMMICAN

¶ 1—8″ square pan

Chewy fruit-nut bars, high in protein and good for eating on the trail or in your tent when it's pocket-food weather.

¶ 1 cup raisins
¶ ½ cup honey
¶ ½ cup milk powder
¶ ½ cup wheat germ
¶ ⅓ cup soy flour
¶ ¼ cup wheat bran
¶ ½ cup each almonds, walnuts, brazils or filberts, whole or chopped
¶ 2 tablespoons corn oil
¶ enough grape or apple juice to make thick batter

Mix all ingredients well. Spread into 8-inch square pan. Bake at 300° for 30 to 40 minutes or until firm. Cut into squares but allow to cool before removing from pan.

VARIATION: add dates or chopped apricots.

RAW GRANOLA

¶ approximately 4 cups

Serve as is with milk, fruit juice, or hot tea. Or for a hot cereal, mix in boiling water.

¶ 1 cup rolled oats, chopped fine
¶ 1 cup rolled wheat, chopped fine
¶ ½ cup almonds, chopped small
¶ ½ cup filberts, chopped small
¶ ½ cup wheat germ
¶ ½ cup unsweetened coconut shreds
¶ ½ cup dry apples, chopped small
¶ ½ cup raisins
¶ 2 tablespoons bran flakes
¶ 2 tablespoons dry grated lemon peel
¶ 1 tablespoon rose hip powder (optional)

Combine all ingredients. Store in covered jar.

GRANOLA BARS

¶ 2—8″ square pans

Chewy, sweet, filling, satisfying, easy to pack, and good for your low energy.

Follow Granola recipe, using 6 cups rolled grains instead of 9. Press into two 8-inch square pans and bake at 300° for 30 to 40 minutes or until golden brown. Cut while hot, but cool before removing from pan.

GRANOLA

¶ approximately 1 gallon

Serve this granola with stewed fruit, hot or cold milk, water, mint or rose hip tea, or just plain dry as a pocket food.

¶ ½ cup oil
¶ ½ cup honey
¶ ½ cup sorghum, molasses or maple syrup
¶ 1 tablespoon vanilla
¶ ¼ cup milk powder
¶ 2 tablespoons nutritional yeast
¶ 1 cup wheat germ
¶ 5 cups rolled oats
¶ 2 cups rolled wheat
¶ 2 cups rolled rye
¶ 1 cup unsweetened coconut shreds
¶ 2 cups raisins or currants
¶ 1 cup each cashews, almonds, pitted dates, sunflower seeds

Heat oil, honey, and syrup in a large pot until thin. Remove from heat. Add remaining ingredients in order given, except fruit, nuts, and seeds. Stir well after each addition. Spread mixture onto a cookie sheet. Bake at 250° for 1½ to 2 hours, stirring occasionally. Cool. Stir in remaining ingredients. Store in airtight container.

CHEESE COOKIES

¶ approximately 2 dozen

¶ ½ pound medium cheddar cheese, grated
¶ 1 cup whole wheat flour
¶ 3 tablespoons oil
¶ ¼ teaspoon salt
¶ dash cayenne
¶ ⅓ cup finely chopped pecans or walnuts, or
   save whole to put on top
¶ 3 to 4 tablespoons milk

Mix grated cheese, flour, oil, salt, and cayenne until an even crumbly texture. Add milk and chopped nuts and knead into a large ball. Roll into balls about 1 inch in diameter and mash between palms of hands. If you didn't add nuts to mixture, place one half nut meat into center top of each cookie. Bake at 350° on oiled cookie sheet for 20 minutes.

HIGH PROTEIN ALMOND COOKIES

¶ approximately 3 dozen

¶ 2¼ cups whole wheat flour
¶ 1 cup almond meal
¶ ¾ cup oat flour
¶ ½ cup chopped pecans
¶ ¼ cup soy flour
¶ ¼ to ½ cup currants or raisins
¶ 2 tablespoons chia seeds
¶ 1 teaspoon coriander
¶ ½ teaspoon salt
¶ ½ cup apple juice or water
¶ ½ cup honey
¶ ¼ cup oil
¶ 1 teaspoon almond extract

Mix all dry ingredients in one bowl and the liquid ingredients in another. Combine the two and blend well. Roll into balls, place on ungreased cookie sheet and press down with a fork. Bake at 350° for 15 to 20 minutes.

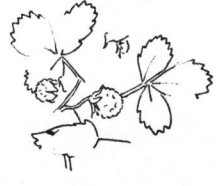

SESAME SEED COOKIES

¶ approximately 2 dozen

Crunchy, satisfying, and high in protein.

¶ 1   cup sesame seeds
¶ ½   cup coconut, grated or shredded
¶ 2   eggs
¶ ½   cup oil
¶ ½   cup honey
¶ 1   teaspoon vanilla
¶ 2¼   cups whole wheat flour
¶ ½   teaspoon salt

Toast sesame seeds and coconut until light
brown. Combine wet ingredients (egg, oil, honey,
and vanilla), then add the toasted seeds and
coconut. Blend in flour and salt and stir well.
Form into balls about 1 inch in diameter and
place on cookie sheet. Press down with fork and
bake at 325° for 15 minutes.

PEANUT BUTTER FUDGE

¶ approximately 1 pound

¶ 1 cup crunchy peanut butter
¶ ½ cup soy milk powder or regular milk
       powder
¶ ½ cup raisins
¶ ¼ cup sesame seeds
¶ ⅛ cup wheat germ
¶ ⅛ to ¼ cup honey

Mix all ingredients together until thoroughly
blended. Carry in lidded plastic container and
break off pieces as you wish.

CASHEW FUDGE

¶ approximately ¾ pound

¶ ½ cup cashew butter
¶ ½ cup chopped cashews
¶ ¼ cup currants or chopped raisins
¶ ¼ cup soy milk powder *or* ½ cup wheat germ
        flakes
¶ 2 tablespoons honey

Combine all ingredients. Carry in lidded plastic
container.

SEED DATE FUDGE

¶ approximately 1¼ pounds

¶ ½ cup sesame seeds
¶ ½ cup sunflower seeds
¶ 1 tablespoon flax seeds
¶ 1 cup chopped dates
¶ ½ cup sesame butter
¶ 2 tablespoons chia seeds
¶ ¼ cup maple syrup (optional)

Grind sesame, sunflower, and flax seeds, or blend
to a meal in a blender. Combine with remaining
ingredients and mix well with hands. Carry in
lidded plastic container.

SESAME BUTTER FUDGE

¶ approximately 1 pound

¶ 1 cup sesame butter
¶ ½ cup almonds, ground fine
¶ ¼ cup honey
¶ handful currants or raisins

Combine all ingredients; knead well. Carry in plastic container with lid.

APRICOT DATE FUDGE

¶ approximately 1½ pounds

¶ 1 cup apricots
¶ 1 cup dates
¶ 1 cup walnuts or pecans
¶ handful raisins or currants
¶ 2 tablespoons wheat germ flakes
¶ 1 cup coconut
¶ juice from ½ lime or lemon

Put fruit, nuts, and wheat germ through a food grinder. Knead in coconut and lime juice until all is mixed well. Carry in lidded plastic container.

SESAME ALMOND FUDGE

¶ approximately 1 pound

¶ 1 cup sesame seeds
¶ ½ cup almonds
¶ ½ cup cashew butter or peanut butter
¶ ¼ cup currants or chopped raisins
¶ 2 tablespoons honey
¶ 1 tablespoon or more water

Grind sesame seeds and almonds to a meal in a nut grinder or blender. Add rest of ingredients, mix well, and pack in lidded plastic container.

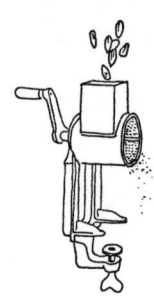

CAROB FUDGE

¶ approximately ½ pound

¶ 1 cup sesame meal or sunflower meal
¶ 2 tablespoons carob powder
¶ 2 tablespoons honey
¶ 1 tablespoon water

Mix all ingredients well in bowl. Pack in lidded plastic container and pinch off pieces as you want them.

VARIATIONS: add ¼ cup coconut; add ½ cup currants or chopped raisins.

PECAN FUDGE

¶ approximately 1¾ pounds

¶ ½ cup honey
¶ ½ cup peanut butter
¶ ½ cup rolled oats (may be chopped or blended in blender)
¶ ½ cup unsweetened coconut
¶ ½ cup chopped pecans
¶ 2 tablespoons soy flour
¶ 1 tablespoon wheat germ flakes
¶ handful peanuts, sunflower seeds, and sesame seeds (may be chopped or ground)
¶ ½ cup honey
¶ 2 teaspoons vanilla
¶ 1 teaspoon lemon juice

Mix in order: honey, peanut butter, oats, coconut, pecans, soy flour, wheat germ flakes, nuts and seeds, vanilla, and lemon juice. Knead a little. Carry in lidded plastic container.

DATE FIG FUDGE

¶ approximately ½ pound

¶ 1 cup dates, pitted
¶ 8 figs
¶ ½ cup walnuts or pecans

Put ingredients through a food grinder and pack in container with lid.

SPREADS AND DRESSINGS

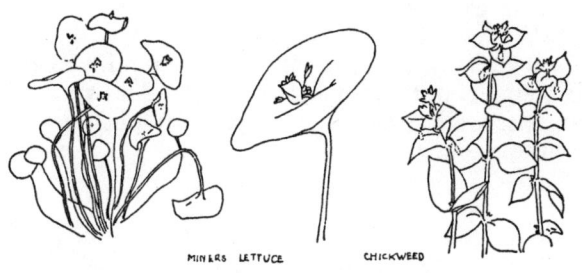

MINERS LETTUCE   CHICKWEED

It's a good idea to prepare these before you go, making for less mess in camp. The spreads are good for any meal, especially lunch, when you usually don't want to cook. The dressings are for a lucky find of wild greens and add extra nourishment to the salad.

BONGKO BEAN SPREAD

A spicy, high energy spread that is good on bread or crackers or as a dip for corn chips.

¶ 1¼ cup cooked garbanzo beans
¶ ¼ teaspoon parsley
¶ ¼ teaspoon chili powder
¶ ⅛ teaspoon cumin
¶ ⅛ teaspoon salt
¶ dash garlic granules

Mash garbanzos or put through a food mill, ricer, or blender, until they make a paste. Add spices and stir well. Store in airtight heavy plastic container.

MISO SESAME BUTTER SPREAD

¶ approximately ¾ cup

High protein, quick energy. Good on crackers, cold leftover pancakes, or bread for lunch.

¶ ¾ cup sesame butter
¶ 2 tablespoons miso
¶ 2 to 3 tablespoons boiling water
¶ grated orange peel (optional)

Brown sesame butter and miso together in frying pan, stirring all the while. Add enough water and mix to make spreading consistency. Cool in bowl. Add orange peel when cool. Store in lidded plastic container.

SESAME BUTTER SPREAD

¶ ½ cup

¶   ½ cup raw sesame butter
¶   dash salt
¶   grated orange peel (optional)

Roast sesame butter and salt in fry pan until brown, stirring all the while, about 5 to 10 minutes in all. Add orange peel when cool.

MISO SPREAD

¶ serves two

Use on breads as a thin spread with or without sliced cheese. This spread is easy to make in camp, too.

¶   3   to 4 cloves garlic, chopped very fine, *or* 5 to 6 wild onions with greens, sliced
¶   2   tablespoons water
¶   1   tablespoon sesame or peanut butter
¶   1   teaspoon miso
¶   ¼   teaspoon olive oil (enough to just cover bottom of pan)

Put oil in fry pan, add garlic or onions. Stir lightly until it turns somewhat translucent. Add mixed miso, peanut or sesame butter, and water and stir for a couple of minutes until it thickens.

VARIATION: for condiment, serve a small amount of spread beside rice or other grain for extra flavor and nourishment.

MIXED SEED BUTTER [SWEET]

¶ approximately 1¾ cups

May be used on bread, crackers, chapatis, or add a little more water and spread on pancakes.

¶ ½ cup pumpkin seeds
¶ ½ cup sunflower seeds
¶ ¼ cup sesame butter
¶ 2 tablespoons honey
¶ 1 tablespoon sesame oil
¶ 1 tablespoon water (approximate)

In seed grinder or blender, grind pumpkin and sunflower seeds. Combine all ingredients in bowl and mix well. Store in airtight heavy plastic container.

VARIATION: to make a Salty Mixed Seed Butter, follow the same recipe, except instead of honey add 2 teaspoons miso and increase the amount of water to approximately 3 tablespoons.

SESAME BUTTER DRESSING

Salad dressings taste really good in the mountains. Not only are they good on salads and steamed greens, but if you prefer you can make a pot of noodles with a small amount of water and add lots of dried parsley and onions, remove from the heat, let cool, and stir in some dressing. This may also be done with boiled or baked potatoes, adding some dill or other herbs.

¶ 1 tablespoon sesame or peanut butter
¶ 2 to 3 teaspoons water
¶ 1 teaspoon tamari soy sauce
¶ 1 teaspoon lemon juice
¶ ½ teaspoon chervil, dill or tarragon

Put all ingredients in a small bottle, shake well, and put in your pack.

MISO SALAD DRESSING

It's easy to mix up a small amount of salad dressing before you go, put it in a jar, and carry it in your pack, ready to use. This recipe has added nourishment because of the miso and it keeps well.

¶ 1 teaspoon each miso, oil, water, and lemon
      juice
¶ 1 clove garlic, sliced
¶ ½ teaspoon whole oregano, thyme, or basil

Put in small bottle or jar and shake well.

FRESH FOODS

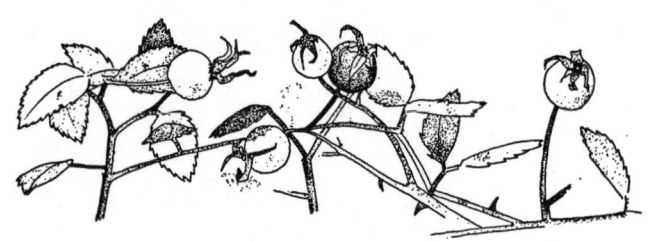

BRING ALONG:
cucumbers, potatoes, onions,
garlic, cabbage, carrots, lemons,
oranges, corn-on-the-cob

FIND ALONG THE TRAIL:
sorrel, dandelion, miners lettuce,
chickweed, watercress, onions,
wild rice, mint, chicory, plantain,
fennel, anise, caraway, rose hips,
asparagus, pine nuts

A small amount of fresh food is a treat when added to the usual dry diet of backpacking. The foods listed above keep well and go a long way. However, for snow camping, we do not recommend taking fresh foods along, except for oranges which you can eat the first day or so. When collecting wild foods, remember not to take the first ones you find (as there may not be any more), never to take more than you need, and to appreciate the plant for its life-giving energy.

Carrots, onions, and cabbage are good for stew and cucumbers for salad. Lemons, onions, and garlic have many possibilities and we recommend taking a lot of them along. Potatoes are good baked in the coals or fried for breakfast. Baking them at home first makes them quick-cooking to add to soup or salad, and lighter in weight to carry. Chopping up vegetables at home, maybe just odds and ends left in your refrigerator, combining them with cheese and herbs, and wrapping first in foil and then in a plastic bag makes a delicious supper to bake in the coals the first night in camp.

BAKED EGGPLANT PARMESAN

An easy meal for the first night out. Prepare for baking at home and pop in the coals when making camp.

¶ 1 unpeeled eggplant, chopped small
¶ ½ pound mushrooms, sliced
¶ 1 onion, chopped
¶ 1 green pepper, sliced
¶ 1 tomato, sliced (optional)
¶ 1 clove garlic, sliced
¶ parsley, chopped
¶ ½ teaspoon oregano
¶ ½ teaspoon basil
¶ ½ teaspoon dill weed
¶ salt and pepper to taste
¶ 1 to 2 cups grated mozzarella, cheddar, Swiss or Jack cheese
¶ ½ cup Parmesan cheese, grated
¶ 2 tablespoons butter

Combine vegetables and herbs and place in the center of a large piece of foil. Dot with butter and sprinkle on cheese. Wrap well and carry in a plastic bag. In camp, make a good fire and rake up a bed of coals, keeping a small fire going along-side. Put foil-wrapped meal in frying pan and nestle in the coals. Bake for 30 minutes. This can also be cooked without the pan on a grate over a very slow fire.

BAKED POTATOES AND MUSHROOMS

¶ serves two

If you collect wild mushrooms, this makes a delicious supper to fix in camp when the mushrooms are at their best. *Be absolutely sure you pick the right ones.* If you have *any hesitation* about wild mushrooms, however, prepare this at home as you would Baked Eggplant Parmesan, using half a pound of domestic mushrooms.

¶ 2 cups chopped wild mushrooms or ½ pound chopped domestic mushrooms
¶ 2 potatoes with skins on, chopped
¶ 1 onion, chopped
¶ parsley or chopped wild greens to taste
¶ 2 garlic cloves, sliced
¶ 2 tablespoons butter
¶ salt, pepper to taste

Combine ingredients and place on foil. Dot with butter and wrap well. Place in frying pan and bake in the coals for 30 to 45 minutes.

EAST INDIAN CORN

A friend brought this idea back from her travels. It's good along with fresh trout, with any meal, or by itself as a snack.

¶ 2 ears of corn, husks removed
¶ 1 lemon
¶ 1 teaspoon salt, mixed with
¶ ½ teaspoon cayenne

Roast huskless corn over hot coals until browned. Rub lemon in salt mixture and then rub on corn.

OTHER WAYS TO COOK CORN

With husks on, soak in stream or salt water for a few minutes and steam over hot coals.

Remove husks and poke on a stick and roast over open fire.

Place in foil with butter and herbs and bake in coals.

Two monks, one older than the other, were traveling in a remote mountain region, visiting from temple to temple. They had heard of a great master living in a temple, high up on the mountain, and started out on the trail to visit him. Just as they were turning up towards the temple, a lettuce leaf came floating down the creek. The young monk exclaimed at the waste and questioned the greatness of the master. Just as he did so, the tenzo (head cook) came running down over boulders and grass with beard and robes flying, pursuing the lost lettuce leaf.

2.

Foods to Make in Camp

Each day is different from the next. Each fire varies in heat. Each camp differs in elevation. We have allowed for these changes in our cooking times.

CEREALS

High protein grains and protein combinations, nuts, dried fruit, and butter all appear in these energizing breakfast cereal recipes.

In winter, when using more energy to keep warm and to keep your endurance level up, you may want to expand your breakfast with one of the following:

a chunk of cheese while you wait for the cereal to cook

nut or seed butters in your cereal or on bread

almond or cashew meal added to cereal

soy, cashew, or almond milk

extra amounts of dried fruits and nuts in cereal

addition of soy grits or millet before cooking

wheat germ and nutritional yeast added after cooking

SEED CEREAL

¶ approximately 2½ cups

Good by itself with cold or warm milk, or serve with Stewed Fruit. May also be used as a high protein garnish for hot cereals.

¶ 1 cup almonds
¶ ½ cup pumpkin seeds
¶ ½ cup sunflower seeds
¶ ¼ cup date sugar
¶ 2 tablespoons carob powder (optional)

Grind nuts and seeds in nut grinder or blender. Combine all ingredients and stir well.

SOAKED CEREAL

¶ serves two to three

¶ 1 cup rolled oats
¶ 1 cup rolled wheat
¶ raisins
¶ coconut
¶ dried apples, chopped
¶ 3 cups water

Mix all ingredients and let soak overnight. Serve for breakfast warm or cold, with or without honey.

VARIATIONS: add chopped nuts; add dried apricots, dates, or other fruit; mix ⅔ cup milk powder with water and add; add cinnamon or other spices; try it with rolled barley or rye; add sesame or sunflower seeds.

BIRD SEED CEREAL

¶ serves two

This cereal has the unique flavor of raw whole grains. The texture is crunchy and chewy.

¶   ¼ cup rolled oats
¶   ¼ cup millet
¶   ¼ cup soy milk powder
¶   ¼ cup almonds or filberts, chopped large
¶   2 tablespoons rolled wheat
¶   2 tablespoons toasted buckwheat groats
¶   small handful raisins, chopped dates, and
          sunflower seeds
¶   pinch salt
¶   1 cup water
¶   date sugar (optional)

Combine all dry ingredients with water in pan the night before in camp. Next morning may be eaten cold or warmed up, stirring often. You might like to sprinkle date sugar on top.

RICE CREAM CEREAL

¶ serves two

A delicate cereal good for small children. Serve with butter and honey.

¶ ½ cup rice flour, toasted
¶ ½ teaspoon salt
¶ 2 cups water

Combine everything and cook till thick, about 10 minutes.

WHEAT GERM CEREAL

¶ serves two

A good breakfast cereal to keep you moving.

¶ ½ cup wheat germ flakes
¶ ½ cup bran flakes
¶ ¼ teaspoon salt
¶ 2 cups water

Mix all ingredients. Simmer 5 minutes.

VARIATIONS: serve with honey or dried fruit (dates are especially good); add ½ cup rolled oats and 1 cup more water; add nuts.

COLD MORNING WHEAT CEREAL

¶ serves two

The dried fruit makes this cereal sweet and the butter helps keep you warm.

- ¶ 1 cup cracked wheat or bulgar
- ¶ ¼ cup milk powder
- ¶ ½ teaspoon salt
- ¶ handful raisins or pitted dates
- ¶ handful walnuts
- ¶ 2 tablespoons butter
- ¶ 4 cups water

Mix wheat, milk, butter, salt, and water. Bring to a boil, then simmer 10 to 15 minutes, stirring occasionally. Add fruit and nuts during last few minutes of cooking. For variety, add chopped dried apples at the beginning of cooking.

OATS AND GROATS

¶ ½ cup rolled oats
¶ ½ cup toasted buckwheat groats
¶ ½ cup (approximately) chopped dried
    apricots
¶ honey
¶ butter
¶ 3 cups water

Combine all ingredients except butter and honey.
Bring to simmer and cook slowly for 15 minutes.
Stir in butter and honey to taste and serve hot.

HOT CRACKED MILLET CREAM CEREAL

¶ serves two

A good winter cereal, high in protein and a source of calcium and iron.

- ¶ ⅔ cup cracked millet (crack in blender or food grinder)
- ¶ ⅔ cup dates
- ¶ ½ cup black walnuts, filberts, or almonds, chopped large
- ¶ ¼ teaspoon salt
- ¶ 2 teaspoons sesame oil or butter (optional)
- ¶ coconut (optional)
- ¶ 2 cups water

Bring all ingredients to a boil, stirring often. Put over low fire and simmer 8 to 10 minutes. Sprinkle top with coconut if you like, and serve with or without milk.

BULGAR CORN MEAL CEREAL

¶ serves two

¶ ⅓ cup corn meal
¶ ¼ cup bulgar
¶ ⅓ cup chopped dried apricots or peaches or currants or raisins
¶ ¼ teaspoon salt
¶ 1 tablespoon butter
¶ 1⅔ cup water

TOPPING

¶ 1 tablespoon toasted sesame seeds
¶ 1 tablespoon date sugar
¶ ⅛ teaspoon cinnamon

Mix topping together and put in separate bag. Combine water, butter, and dry ingredients in first list and stir well. Bring to boil and simmer for 15 minutes, stirring occasionally. When done, sprinkle on topping and serve.

PANCAKES

Pancakes are good for slow
mornings, when you feel like
sitting in the sun on a granite
boulder with a cup of hot tea,
letting it all soak in and warm you
up after a frosty night.
Cook extra and save as bread
for lunch.

OATMEAL HOTCAKES

Good for mornings when you want to eat a lot.
These are sweet and filling.

¶ 2 cups oatmeal (whir in blender or grind
until most of it is a flourlike consistency,
with some of it still in small pieces)
¶ ½ cup milk powder
¶ ¼ teaspoon cinnamon
¶ ¼ teaspoon nutmeg
¶ ¼ teaspoon salt
¶ ¼ cup date sugar (optional)
¶ ¼ cup currants or raisins
¶ 1 tablespoon sesame seeds
¶ 1½ cups water

All dry ingredients may be kept in one bag. In
camp the night before, combine ingredients with
water in a bowl, cover, and let soak overnight.
The next morning, make large cakes, about 3
inches across and ¾ inch thick, and fry slowly in
a little oil. Very good with maple syrup or Honey
Syrup and butter.

CORN PANCAKES

Good with peanut butter and maple syrup or
Stewed Fruit.

- ¶ 1 cup corn flour or corn meal
- ¶ ½ cup whole wheat flour
- ¶ ½ cup wheat germ
- ¶ ½ cup milk powder
- ¶ ½ teaspoon salt
- ¶ 1 tablespoon honey
- ¶ 2 tablespoons oil
- ¶ 1½ cups water

Combine dry ingredients. Add water, oil and
honey and mix well. Bake on hot, oiled fry pan;
save leftovers for lunch.

BUCKWHEAT PANCAKES

¶ serves two to four

- ¶ 1 cup buckwheat flour
- ¶ ½ cup whole wheat flour
- ¶ ½ cup corn meal
- ¶ ½ cup wheat germ
- ¶ ½ cup milk powder
- ¶ 2 teaspoons baking powder (optional)
- ¶ 1 teaspoon salt
- ¶ 2 tablespoons oil
- ¶ 2 to 3 cups water

Pack all dry ingredients in one bag at home before you go. In camp, add oil and enough water to make a thick batter. If not using baking powder, make batter thinner. Bake on moderately hot oiled surface.

VARIATION: add wild berries, raisins, or dried bananas, chopped small.

WHOLE WHEAT SOY PANCAKES

¶ serves two

Good, heavy pancakes, very high in protein and energy. They come out dark and are delicious with maple syrup.

- ¶ 2 cups whole wheat flour
- ¶ ½ cup soy flour
- ¶ ½ cup wheat germ flakes
- ¶ ½ cup milk powder
- ¶ 2 teaspoons baking powder (optional)
- ¶ 1 teaspoon salt
- ¶ ½ cup oil
- ¶ 2 cups water

Combine dry ingredients. Stir in liquids. Cook on oiled frying pan over medium heat.

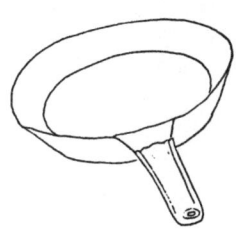

BROWN RICE FLOUR PANCAKES

¶ serves two

A light, mellow pancake. Good with sesame butter and honey or maple syrup.

¶ 2 cups brown rice flour
¶ ⅓ cup milk powder
¶ 2 teaspoons baking powder (optional)
¶ ½ teaspoon salt
¶ 2 tablespoons honey
¶ ¼ cup oil
¶ 1 cup water

Combine dry ingredients. Mix in honey, oil, and water. Bake in moderately hot pan until browned on both sides and springy to the touch.

SOUPS

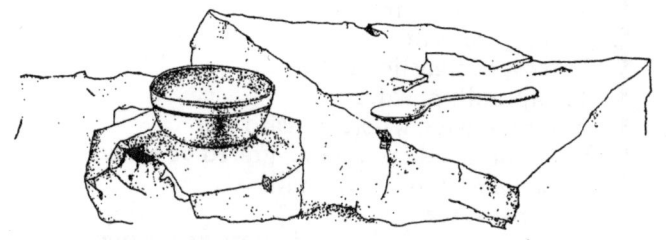

We have found that it is easy and satisfying to package our own soup mixes—controlling what goes in them, keeping the cost down, and making taste changes and nutritional supplements. All of these soups are intended for quick lunches or a light addition to your evening meal while you're waiting for the main course to cook, or for those times when you just want a quick cup of soup. You might want to add vegetable bouillon cubes to some of these recipes for added strength.

SPINACH CHEESE SOUP

A single recipe serves two for lunch or before a main course for supper. Doubled, it serves two for supper along with crackers or journey cakes.

¶ 2 tablespoons spinach flakes
¶ 1 tablespoon onion flakes
¶ 1 tablespoon parsley flakes
¶ ½ teaspoon salt
¶ ⅛ teaspoon garlic granules
¶ ½ cup milk powder
¶ 2 tablespoons whole wheat flour
¶ ½ pound cheddar cheese, grated or sliced
¶ 1 tablespoon oil (optional)
¶ 3 cups water
¶ handful toasted chopped almonds (optional)

Package first 5 ingredients in one bag and milk powder and whole wheat flour in another. In camp, mix 2 cups water, oil, and first bag. Bring to boil, and cook 5 minutes. Meanwhile, stir together milk, flour, and remaining 1 cup water. Add to soup broth and stir in grated cheese. Do not boil. Stir until cheese melts. Sprinkle on almonds. Serve hot.

FIVE-GRAIN SOUP

¶ serves two

A filling creamy soup, and quick-cooking. Very good for rainy-day lunch in the tent. Serve with cheese or peanut butter and crackers.

¶ 3 tablespoons rolled oats
¶ 2 tablespoons dehydrated diced potato or 1 baked potato, chopped small
¶ 1 tablespoon whole wheat flour
¶ 1 tablespoon barley flour
¶ 1 tablespoon millet flour
¶ 1 tablespoon rye flour
¶ 1 tablespoon nutritional yeast (optional)
¶ 1 tablespoon milk powder
¶ 1 tablespoon dehydrated carrots
¶ 1 teaspoon onion flakes
¶ 1 teaspoon parsley flakes
¶ ¾ teaspoon salt
¶ dash garlic granules
¶ 1 teaspoon oil
¶ 4 cups water

Combine all ingredients in cold water and oil. Bring to a boil, stirring frequently. After soup comes to a boil, place on low fire and let it bubble gently for 5 minutes.

PEANUT BUTTER SOUP

¶ serves two

- ¶ 2 tablespoons onion flakes
- ¶ 2 tablespoons whole wheat flour
- ¶ ½ teaspoon salt
- ¶ ¼ teaspoon celery seed
- ¶ ¼ teaspoon pepper
- ¶ 1 bay leaf
- ¶ 2 tablespoons butter
- ¶ ½ cup milk powder
- ¶ 2 tablespoons Parmesan cheese
- ¶ ½ cup peanut butter
- ¶ 4 cups water

Package first six ingredients in one bag and the milk powder and cheese in a separate one. In camp, put butter in soup pan and melt. Add onion, flour, salt, celery seed, pepper, and bay leaf and stir well. When flour starts to stick to bottom, add 3 cups water, stir well, and bring to a boil. In the meantime, mix 1 cup water, milk powder, and Parmesan cheese. As soon as mixture on fire boils, add peanut butter and stir it in well. Then add milk mixture and stir again. Bring this to a boil and simmer for 5 to 10 minutes. May be served with soya-bacon bits on top. May be eaten hot or cold.

CLAM CHOWDER

¶ ½ cup dehydrated diced potato or 1 raw
   unpeeled potato chopped very small
¶ 1 teaspoon dill weed
¶ ¼ teaspoon salt
¶ 1 garlic clove, minced, or ⅛ teaspoon garlic
   granules
¶ ¼ cup milk powder
¶ 2 tablespoons whole wheat flour
¶ 1 6½-ounce can minced clams with juice
¶ 1 teaspoon oil
¶ 4 cups water

Combine 3 cups water, oil, potato, dill, salt, and
garlic. Simmer 10 minutes. Meanwhile, mix milk
powder and flour with clam juice and enough
cold water to make 1 cup. Stir well, and add to
soup broth along with clams. Heat through, but do
not boil.

TOMATO NOODLE SOUP

A flavorful tomato soup, very good with journey
cakes or garlic bread with a chunk of cheese
on the side.

¶ 1   cup freeze-dried tomato powder
¶ 6   ounces whole-grain or vegetable noodles
¶ ¼   cup nutritional yeast
¶ 2   teaspoons onion flakes
¶ 2   teaspoons parsley flakes
¶ 1   teaspoon oregano
¶ 1   teaspoon salt
¶ 1   tablespoon wheat germ oil
¶ 3½ cups water

Combine ingredients and bring to boil, stirring
often. High simmer for 10 minutes.

GARNISHES: wheat germ flakes; Parmesan
cheese; wild onions, sliced fine; wild greens,
chopped; toasted sesame seeds; squeeze of lemon.

POTATO CHEESE SOUP

¶ ½ cup dehydrated potato pieces or 1 unpeeled baked potato, chopped small
¶ ½ cup milk powder
¶ 2 tablespoons oat flour
¶ 2 tablespoons whole wheat flour
¶ 1 tablespoon onion flakes
¶ 1 tablespoon wheat germ flakes
¶ 1 teaspoon parsley flakes
¶ ½ teaspoon salt
¶ dash pepper
¶ ½ pound grated Parmesan or cheddar cheese, cut in chunks
¶ 1 tablespoon oil
¶ 4 cups water

Put all ingredients except cheese in cold water and oil. Stir well. Bring to boil, stirring all the while. Simmer approximately 5 to 10 minutes, stirring from time to time. Remove from heat, add cheese, stir well. Serve hot.

MINESTRONE

- ¶ ½ cup noodles
- ¶ ½ cup freeze-dried navy, pinto, or kidney beans
- ¶ ¼ cup tomato powder or vegetable broth powder
- ¶ ¼ cup Parmesan cheese, grated
- ¶ 2 tablespoons parsley flakes
- ¶ 1 tablespoon dehydrated spinach flakes (optional)
- ¶ 1 teaspoon onion flakes or 1 small onion, chopped
- ¶ 1 teaspoon celery flakes
- ¶ 1 teaspoon salt
- ¶ 1 garlic clove or ⅛ teaspoon garlic granules
- ¶ ½ teaspoon basil
- ¶ ½ teaspoon oregano
- ¶ 1 teaspoon olive oil or safflower oil
- ¶ 4 cups water

Bring water and oil to boil. Add all dry ingredients, and bring to boil again, stirring occasionally. Reduce heat and let simmer 10 minutes longer.

CREAM OF MUSHROOM SOUP

¶ serves two

Good winter soup; strong mushroom flavor, thick and creamy.

¶ ⅓ cup dried mushrooms, sliced thin and chopped fine, or 1½ cups wild mushrooms, sliced fine
¶ ⅓ cup milk powder
¶ 2 tablespoons whole wheat flour
¶ 2 teaspoons nutritional yeast
¶ 2 teaspoons wheat germ flakes
¶ 1 teaspoon onion flakes
¶ 1 teaspoon parsley flakes
¶ 1 teaspoon salt
¶ dash nutmeg
¶ dash pepper
¶ 1 teaspoon oil
¶ 4 cups water

Put all ingredients in cold water and oil, and stirring frequently, bring to boil. When it comes to a boil, put on lower heat and simmer for 10 minutes longer, stirring occasionally.

SPINACH CLAM SOUP

- ¶ 1 cup dehydrated spinach
- ¶ 1 teaspoon onion flakes
- ¶ 1 teaspoon parsley flakes
- ¶ ⅛ teaspoon garlic granules
- ¶ ⅛ teaspoon thyme
- ¶ ⅛ teaspoon basil
- ¶ dash nutmeg
- ¶ dash pepper
- ¶ ½ cup milk powder
- ¶ 1 6½-ounce can clams and juice
- ¶ ½ teaspoon lemon juice (optional)
- ¶ 3½ cups water
- ¶ 1 tablespoon butter
- ¶ Parmesan cheese and/or chopped almonds as garnish

At home, bag first 8 ingredients together. In camp, bring 3 cups water and butter to a boil. Add all dry ingredients except milk powder and Parmesan cheese. Bring to boil and simmer 5 minutes. Meanwhile, mix ½ cup water and milk powder. Add to soup when done and stir well. Add lemon juice, if used, and clams and heat through. Do not boil. Serve with Parmesan cheese or chopped almonds sprinkled on top.

nOODLE SOUP

¶ serves two

- ¶ 6 ounces noodles, spinach, sesame, or soy
- ¶ ¼ cup dried mushrooms, sliced thin and chopped fine
- ¶ 1 tablespoon onion flakes
- ¶ 1 tablespoon vegetable-seasoned broth powder
- ¶ 1 tablespoon parsley flakes
- ¶ ½ teaspoon oregano
- ¶ ½ teaspoon salt
- ¶ ¼ teaspoon garlic granules
- ¶ ¼ teaspoon pepper
- ¶ 1 tablespoon olive oil
- ¶ 4 cups water
- ¶ 1 teaspoon tamari soy sauce

Bring water and oil to boil. Add all other ingredients, and bring to boil again. Cover and keep at a high simmer for 10 minutes. Add tamari at end.

GARNISHES: squeeze of lemon; Parmesan or romano cheese, grated; toasted sesame seeds; fresh wild onions, sliced very fine.

TOMATO CORN SOUP

Very good with broken bits of raw cheddar cheese dropped in while hot, just before serving.

¶ ½ cup dehydrated corn
¶ ¼ cup toasted buckwheat groats
¶ ¼ cup tomato powder
¶ 2 tablespoons celery flakes
¶ 1 teaspoon oregano
¶ 1 teaspoon parsley flakes
¶ 1 teaspoon onion flakes
¶ ¾ teaspoon salt
¶ ⅛ teaspoon garlic granules
¶ 1 teaspoon oil
¶ 4 cups water

All dry ingredients may be packed together at home. In camp, pour into cold water and oil and bring to a boil. Simmer for 10 to 15 minutes, just until groats are soft.

BAKED BEAN SOUP

Very good over corn pancakes.

¶ 1¾ cup freeze-dried pinto beans
¶ 2 tablespoons onion flakes
¶ ½ teaspoon salt
¶ ½ teaspoon ginger
¶ 2 tablespoons molasses, honey, or maple
    syrup
¶ 1 tablespoon corn oil
¶ 4 cups water
¶ 1 tablespoon tamari soy sauce

Mix all ingredients together in cook-pot, except
tamari. Bring to boil and cook for 10 to 15
minutes. Add tamari when done.

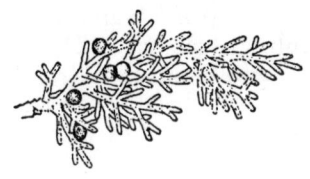

KOMBU FISH BROTH

A good salty broth after a strenuous day. May be served as is or with enough additions to make a complete meal.

¶   4   by 4-inch piece of kombu
¶   3   tablespoons bonita fish flakes *or* handful of
            iriki (small dried fish)
¶   ¼ cup tamari soy sauce
¶   4   cups water

Bring all ingredients to boil except tamari. Move to lower heat and simmer 10 to 15 minutes. Strain (optional). Add tamari.

GARNISHES: chopped sorrel or wild onions; toasted sesame seeds; Parmesan cheese; popcorn.

VARIATIONS: see Seaweed Soup and Watercress Soup; drop in Fish Dumplings (see page 121) after it has come to a boil; add handful of dried shrimp at the beginning or freeze-dried or canned shrimp at the end; add 6 ounces noodles when broth comes to a boil.

SEAWEED SOUP

May be served with Sesame Seed Bread with a nut or seed butter spread on top.

¶ 4 by 4-inch piece of kombu
¶ ¼ cup hiziki (seaweed)
¶ ¼ cup shredded daikon white radish
(optional)
¶ 3 tablespoons bonita fish flakes
¶ 2 tablespoons dried mushrooms, sliced thin
and chopped fine
¶ 1 tablespoon onion flakes
¶ ¼ teaspoon ginger, ground
¶ handful dried shrimp
¶ 5 cups water

Combine all in cook-pot and bring to boil. Keep at a high simmer for 25 to 30 minutes. Sprinkle sesame seeds or onion slices on top.

WATERCRESS SOUP

- ¶ 4 by 4-inch piece of kombu
- ¶ ¼ cup dried mushrooms, sliced thin, chopped fine
- ¶ 3 tablespoons bonita fish flakes
- ¶ 1 tablespoon onion flakes
- ¶ ¼ teaspoon ginger, ground
- ¶ 4 cups water
- ¶ 2 cups (approximately) watercress or sorrel
- ¶ ¼ cup tamari soy sauce

Combine seaweed, fish flakes, mushrooms, onions, and water. Bring to a boil and simmer 10 to 15 minutes. Remove from heat, add greens and tamari and cover 2 to 3 minutes. Serve hot.

VARIATIONS: add 6 ounces noodles at beginning of cooking; drop in Fish Dumplings (see page 121) when broth boils; add canned or freeze-dried shrimp along with greens.

PARTAN BREE— A SCOTTISH SOUP

¶ serves two

A mild, milky soup, light in flavor, for one of those nights when you need something soothing to eat.

¶ ¼ cup brown rice
¶ 1 teaspoon onion flakes
¶ 1 teaspoon parsley flakes
¶ ¼ teaspoon salt
¶ ½ cup milk powder
¶ 2 tablespoons butter
¶ pepper to taste
¶ 1 6½-ounce can crabmeat with juice
¶ 4½ cups water

Combine 2½ cups of the water, rice, onions, parsley, and salt and bring to a boil. Cook for 40 to 45 minutes, or until rice is done. Meanwhile, combine remaining 2 cups water and milk powder in separate bowl or cup. When rice is ready, add milk, crabmeat with juice, butter, and pepper. Warm through, but do not boil again. Serve hot. Sprinkle wheat germ flakes on top in bowls, if desired.

GREEN PEA SOUP WITH SEAWEED GREEN

¶ serves three to four

A light soup that is a surprisingly good combination. Try serving it with Cheese Toasties for a light meal, with popcorn for dessert.

¶ 1½ cups green split peas
¶ ¼ cup vegetable-seasoned broth powder
¶ 3 by 3-inch square of kombu
¶ ½ teaspoon salt
¶ 1 tablespoon oil
¶ 5 cups water

Bring water to a boil. Add all ingredients and cook at a high simmer for 45 to 50 minutes.

Knap Sack Nap Snack

A resting recipe.

Just stop.

Serves your reserves.

PATTIES

These cakes are made fresh in
camp, after the dry ingredients
have been packaged in one bag at
home. They can form the center of
the evening meal, or accompany
just a bowl of soup. The variety of
things you can put on top includes:
tamari soy sauce, hot mustard,
sweet toppings, sauces, gravies,
nut and seed spreads, and salad
dressings. They are
simple to make.

MEAL CAKES

These cakes will form a brown crust on the outside and inside will slightly steam. Very satisfying in cold weather for breakfast or any time as a dessert after a light supper.

- ¶ ½ cup whole wheat flour
- ¶ ½ cup millet meal
- ¶ ½ cup sunflower seed meal
- ¶ ½ cup almond meal
- ¶ ¼ teaspoon salt
- ¶ 1 cup hot water

Place dry ingredients in a bowl. Add hot water, stir, and let sit for 15 minutes or so, and then form 1 heaping tablespoonful into a ball (dough will be moist) and pat into a pancake shape, about ⅜ inch thick. Cook on lightly greased frying pan. Serve with butter and honey or Date Walnut Topping. Very good cold for later in the day with peanut butter and honey or cold topping. Makes one dozen small cakes.

FOR SUPPER

add to above:

- ¶ 1 cup or so wild greens, chopped very fine
- ¶ 1 medium onion, chopped fine, or 1 tablespoon onion flakes
- ¶ 1 teaspoon savory
- ¶ ½ teaspoon salt (rather than ¼ teaspoon salt)

Cook as above, serve with tamari soy sauce or Peanut Butter Gravy or hot mustard.

FISH PATTIES

¶ 1 9¼-ounce can tuna or albacore or other
    canned fish or 1½ cups leftover cooked
    fish
¶ ¼ cup wheat germ flakes
¶ ¼ cup milk powder
¶ ½ teaspoon basil *or* ¼ teaspoon dill weed
¶ 1 tablespoon oil, if using leftover fish
¶ 1 tablespoon water

Drain oil from canned fish into heating frying
pan, or if using leftover fish, put 1 tablespoon oil
in frying pan. Mix all ingredients in bowl. Form
into 4 patties and pat wheat germ flakes on each
side. Fry slowly, about 10 to 15 minutes, turning
once. Sprinkle on lemon juice, if available, or
make some mustard from dry powder.

VARIATION: You may add leftover cooked grain
to these patties and they will serve four. Simply
double the herb, add ¼ teaspoon salt, and add 1
tablespoon water (this will depend on the
moistness of the grain). Follow as above and serve
with soy sauce or mustard. You may also need to
use more oil when cooking.

SUNFLOWER SEED PATTIES

¶ serves two

A mild sunflower seed flavor, very good with Curry or Mushroom Gravy.

¶ 1 cup sunflower seed meal (may be ground in grinder or blender)
¶ 2 tablespoons oat flour
¶ 1 teaspoon celery flakes
¶ 1 teaspoon parsley flakes
¶ ½ teaspoon chervil
¶ ¼ teaspoon salt
¶ ¼ teaspoon savory
¶ ⅛ teaspoon garlic granules (optional)
¶ 1 teaspoon oil
¶ 2 tablespoons water

Combine all dry ingredients, water, and oil in camp and stir well. Let sit for 5 minutes. Form into 4 small patties, mashed like a thick pancake. Fry in lightly greased frying pan for about 7 minutes per side.

SESAME SEED PATTIES

¶ serves two

Tasty, crunchy hot supper cakes. Good with a sauce, gravy, hot mustard, or just soy sauce.

¶ 1 cup sesame seed meal (ground in grinder or blender)
¶ ¼ cup soy flour
¶ ¼ cup wheat germ flakes
¶ 1 teaspoon onion flakes
¶ 1 teaspoon parsley flakes
¶ 1 teaspoon sage
¶ ¼ teaspoon celery seed
¶ ¼ teaspoon garlic granules
¶ ¼ teaspoon salt
¶ 1 teaspoon oil
¶ ⅓ cup water

Combine all dry ingredients with water and oil in one bowl and stir well. Form into 4 patties and fry in lightly oiled frying pan for about 7 minutes per side.

SOY GRIT PATTIES

¶ serves two

¶ ½ cup soy grits
¶ 1 tablespoon onion flakes
¶ ½ teaspoon oregano
¶ ½ teaspoon parsley flakes
¶ 1 bay leaf
¶ ½ cup whole wheat flour
¶ ¼ teaspoon salt
¶ 1 garlic clove, minced, or ⅛ teaspoon garlic
    granules
¶ 1 cup water
¶ oil enough to fry in

Bring water to boil and slowly sprinkle in grits, onions, and herbs. Cover, and let boil until the water is almost completely absorbed, about 10 minutes. Remove from heat and add remaining ingredients. Let sit for 10 to 15 minutes, covered. Heat enough oil in frying pan to keep from sticking. Remove bay leaf. Form into patties and fry 3 to 4 minutes on each side. Serve with Peanut Butter Gravy, Tomato Sauce, gravy, or just plain soy sauce. Makes approximately 8 small patties.

GRAINS

Here are a few grain recipes that are good with sauces or gravies poured over them or as a complement to freshly caught fish. The leftovers also make good journey cakes. All you have to do is form them into patties, fry them the next morning, and save them in your pack.

PLAIN BROWN RICE

Whole grains take a while to cook, so most people wouldn't think of cooking them in the back country. There's no hurry. Make camp early, put the rice on to simmer, and wander down by the creek to fish or take in the rich golden light of late afternoon. By the time gold turns into the first flush of pink your rice will be done. It's a special feeling sitting by the fire with a steaming bowl of plain brown rice.

¶ 1 cup brown rice
¶ 1 teaspoon salt
¶ 3 cups water

Bring to simmer and steam 30 to 60 minutes, or until all water is absorbed. Millet, bulgar, lentils, and mung beans are good plain, too. Or season with soy sauce, sesame salt, or wild onions. Cook extra and save for breakfast to eat with dried fruit and honey. Or add herbs and wild greens, form into patties, fry and eat for lunch or supper with cheese or a thick sauce or gravy poured over them. Don't forget, combining different grains and beans makes more usable protein per pound, besides tasting really good.

GROATS 'n CORN

¶ ¾ cup dehydrated corn
¶ ½ cup toasted buckwheat groats
¶ 1 large dried mushroom, sliced thin, chopped fine (approximately 2 tablespoons)
¶ 1 tablespoon dried bell pepper
¶ 1 teaspoon onion flakes
¶ 1 teaspoon parsley flakes
¶ 1 teaspoon celery flakes
¶ ½ teaspoon salt
¶ ⅛ teaspoon paprika
¶ 1 tablespoon butter
¶ 3¼ cups water

All dry ingredients may be combined together and packed in one bag. Put everything in cold water and bring to a boil. Simmer for 10 to 15 minutes and serve.

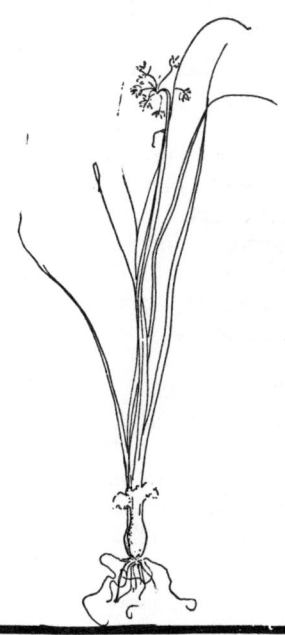

MUSHROOM BULGAR

- ¶ 1¼ cups bulgar
- ¶ ¼ cup dried chopped mushrooms
- ¶ 2 tablespoons onion flakes
- ¶ 1 tablespoon dehydrated carrots
- ¶ 2 teaspoons vegetable-seasoned broth powder
- ¶ 1 teaspoon celery flakes
- ¶ 1 teaspoon parsley flakes
- ¶ ½ teaspoon salt
- ¶ ⅛ teaspoon powdered savory
- ¶ 2 tablespoons oil
- ¶ 3 cups water

Sauté all dry ingredients in oil for 5 minutes. Add water and bring to a boil. Cover and simmer 20 minutes longer.

BULGAR WITH SAGE

¶ serves two

- ¶ 1 cup bulgar or millet
- ¶ 2 tablespoons celery flakes or ¼ teaspoon celery seed
- ¶ 1 tablespoon onion flakes
- ¶ ½ teaspoon salt
- ¶ ¼ teaspoon garlic granules
- ¶ pinch sage and thyme
- ¶ 1 teaspoon oil
- ¶ 3 cups water
- ¶ 2 tablespoons peanut butter

Bring water to a boil, and add everything but peanut butter. Simmer 20 minutes. Stir in peanut butter and heat through.

BUCKWHEAT STEW

¶ serves two

A mellow meal served with Cheese Toasties.

¶ ½ cup raw buckwheat groats
¶ ½ cup dehydrated potato slices or chunks, *or* 1
     fresh potato, diced, or 4 ounces noodles
¶ ½ cup dehydrated cabbage flakes
¶ 2 teaspoons parsley flakes
¶ 1 teaspoon oregano *or* ¼ teaspoon caraway
     seeds
¶ ½ teaspoon salt
¶ 1 teaspoon oil
¶ 3 cups water

Bring water to a boil. Add all ingredients. Simmer
20 minutes.

GARNISHES: grated Parmesan cheese, sesame
salt, toasted sesame seeds, soy sauce.

BUCKWHEAT STRING BEANS

If you get this going and then fry trout on the side, it will probably be done at the same time, offering a satisfying complete meal.

- ¶ 1 cup toasted buckwheat groats
- ¶ ¾ cup dehydrated or ⅓ cup freeze-dried string beans
- ¶ ½ cup dried mushrooms, sliced thin and chopped fine, or if you prefer mushrooms chunky, cut and presoak them for 20 to 30 minutes
- ¶ 1 tablespoon onion flakes
- ¶ ½ teaspoon salt
- ¶ ¼ teaspoon oregano
- ¶ 1 teaspoon oil
- ¶ 3¼ cups water

Slowly add all ingredients to boiling water and oil, keeping the water boiling. Stir, cover, and let cook at a low boil for 20 minutes. Serve with tamari soy sauce or sesame salt.

VARIATION: this could be made a One-Pot Meal by simply adding a handful of dried shrimp at the beginning or a small can of shrimp at the end.

GRAIN SALAD WITH FORAGED GREENS

¶ serves two

This may be made in the morning, left to sit in a creek or the shade until lunch, when you might add fresh chopped greens. A very delicate flavor; good with crackers and cheese.

¶ ¾ cup bulgar
¶ 2 tablespoons onion flakes
¶ 2 tablespoons parsley flakes
¶ 2 teaspoons hiziki seaweed (optional)
¶ ¼ teaspoon salt
¶ 1 clove garlic, minced (optional)
¶ 2 tablespoons oil
¶ 1 teaspoon lemon juice
¶ 1⅓ cups boiling water
¶ fresh greens: sorrel, miners lettuce, dandelion greens, watercress

Place dry ingredients in bowl and add boiling water and oil. Let sit covered for 20 minutes. Add greens, broken into bite-size pieces, lemon juice and garlic. Toss well.

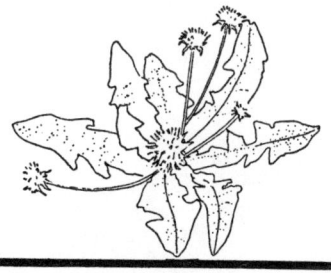

FISH

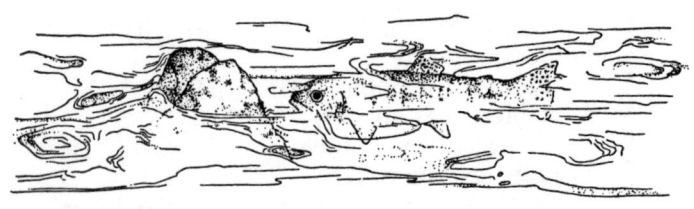

We use trout in all of our fish recipes, as they're the most likely to be caught in our area; however, don't feel limited.

BASIC FRIED TROUT

We always carry a bag of breading mixture for frying trout. Here are a few combinations that we enjoy:

¶ corn meal, salt, pepper, sage (optional) to taste
¶ 1 part corn meal, 1 part corn flour, salt, pepper to taste
¶ whole wheat flour, salt, pepper to taste
¶ whole wheat flour, salt, pepper, garlic granules, sesame seeds to taste

Clean freshly caught fish and while still wet, roll in mixture and fry. Fish will be done when flesh is no longer translucent and flakes away when pried with a fork. Sprinkle on a little lemon juice, if you like.

BEN'S FRIED TROUT

If you're as good a fisherman as Ben Kinmont, and catch plenty of fish along the way, you might like to try his recipe for a different taste.

Wash and clean fresh-caught trout, leaving it a little moist. Sprinkle a combination of garlic granules, salt and pepper on one side, and put that side down in a hot frying pan with a little oil. While cooking, sprinkle more of the same on the other side. Turn, and fry until done.

BAKED TROUT

This is a good recipe for one of the first nights out, when you still might have a baked potato left, and the fishing has been fine.

¶ 4 medium-sized trout, or enough for two
¶ 1 baked fresh potato, chopped fine
¶ ½ teaspoon salt
¶ ⅛ teaspoon pepper
¶ ⅛ teaspoon thyme
¶ ⅛ teaspoon basil
¶ butter
¶ fresh greens, chopped: watercress, sorrel, dandelion, chicory

In small bowl, combine all ingredients except butter and greens. Stuff in and around freshly cleaned trout, laid out on a large piece of foil. Dot with butter and sprinkle in chopped greens. Seal foil and bake in coals for 30 minutes or so.

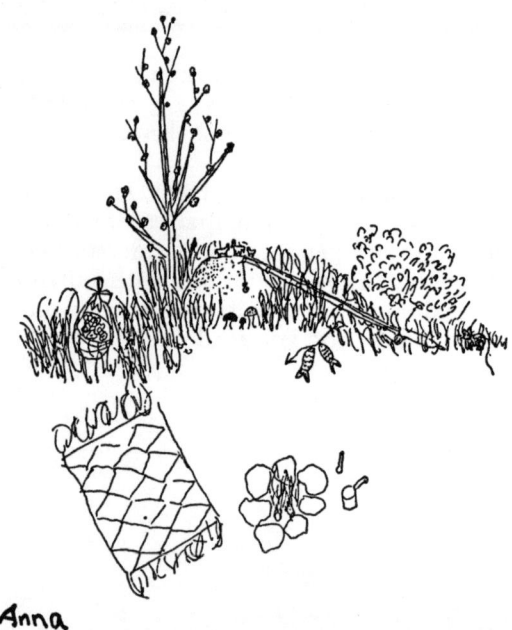

Anna

BAKED TROUT WITH BUCKWHEAT STUFFING

A supper to make when you just know you're gonna catch some. Put the groats on to soak while you fish.

¶ enough fresh trout for two
¶ ½ cup buckwheat groats
¶ 1 cup water
¶ 1 onion, sliced
¶ 1 lemon, sliced
¶ 1 garlic clove, sliced
¶ 1 tablespoon parsley flakes
¶ 1 teaspoon whole oregano
¶ ½ teaspoon dill weed
¶ salt to taste
¶ 1 tablespoon butter

Soak groats in water for 15 minutes and drain off excess water. Combine with onion, garlic, lemon, and seasoning. Rub cleaned fish with half the butter and stuff with groat mixture. Dot with remaining butter, wrap in foil, seal well. Place in coals and bake 30 minutes.

TROUT SOUP

¶ serves two

This recipe is good for those evenings when you want to eat cooked fish in some way besides fried. Either use freshly poached fish (reserving the broth to measure in with the water) or leftovers, already cooked. Even canned fish may be used. Seasonings may be combined in a small packet before going, or along with the dry noodles.

¶ 6 ounces noodles
¶ 1 bay leaf
¶ 1 teaspoon parsley flakes
¶ ½ teaspoon salt
¶ ¼ teaspoon thyme
¶ ⅛ teaspoon celery seed
¶ ⅛ teaspoon sage
¶ dash of pepper
¶ 2 garlic cloves, minced, or ¼ teaspoon garlic granules
¶ 1 cup cooked fish, broken in pieces or flaked
¶ 2 teaspoons olive oil
¶ 4 cups water

Bring water and oil to a boil and add all ingredients except fish. Simmer for 10 minutes or until noodles are done. Add fish and heat through. Sprinkle a small amount of chopped wild greens on top or one finely sliced wild onion, if you happened upon some. You also might like to use a little soy sauce or grated Parmesan cheese on top.

FISH DUMPLINGS

A good addition to a thin soup, such as Miso or Garlic Broth; nourishing and filling.

- ¶ 1 cup cooked or canned flaked fish
- ¶ ½ cup wheat germ flakes
- ¶ ¼ cup garbanzo bean flour
- ¶ ½ teaspoon salt
- ¶ ⅛ teaspoon dill weed *or* pinch nutmeg
- ¶ 2 teaspoons oil
- ¶ 2 tablespoons water

Combine all ingredients in a bowl and mix together well. Between the palms of your hands, roll into balls about 1 inch in diameter. Drop into boiling soup, put pot on lower fire, and simmer 10 minutes. Makes approximately 12 small dumplings.

IRIKI

If you get a chance to go to Chinatown, or to a place where they carry Chinese or Japanese products, you might see these very small dried fish, about 2 inches long. These are very lightweight and a real treat for a snack. They are very high in protein, as the whole fish is eaten, bones and all.

Oil bottom of skillet, put in a handful of dried fish. Brown until toasty and crunchy, sprinkle with soy sauce, and stir a little bit more. Remove from pan and cool on plate.

ONE-POT LUCK

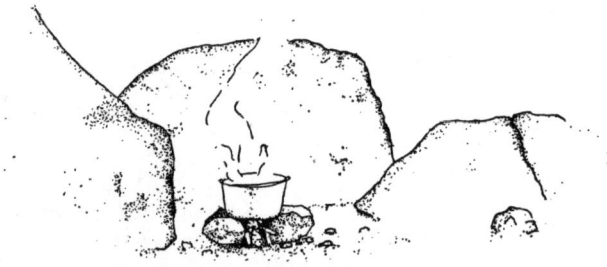

Simple meals to be made in one
pot. All the ingredients are
combined in one bag, thrown in a
pot of water in camp, and take
from 15 to 60 minutes to cook.
They are wholesome, complete
meals, satisfying after a hard day's
work.

Form any leftovers into patties
and fry the next morning for
breakfast or a cold lunch or for the
next supper with a sauce or gravy.

CHILI

Put some cheese in your bowl and pour on some of this chili. Good with cornbread cakes on a cold 10,000-foot night.

¶ 1 cup lentils
¶ 3 tablespoons tomato powder (optional)
¶ 2 tablespoons masa or corn flour (optional)
¶ 1 tablespoon chili powder
¶ 1 tablespoon onion flakes
¶ 1 teaspoon cumin
¶ 1 teaspoon oregano
¶ 1 teaspoon salt
¶ 1 garlic clove or ⅛ teaspoon garlic granules
¶ 4 cups water

Combine all ingredients and simmer 30 to 45 minutes depending on altitude.

POLENTA CHEESE SOUP

¶ ½ cup dehydrated corn
¶ ¼ cup polenta
¶ 1 tablespoon dehydrated bell pepper
¶ 1 bay leaf
¶ 1 teaspoon parsley flakes
¶ 1 teaspoon onion flakes
¶ 1 teaspoon celery flakes
¶ ½ teaspoon salt
¶ ⅛ teaspoon savory
¶ dash cayenne
¶ 1 teaspoon oil
¶ 4 cups water
¶ ½ cup milk powder
¶ ¼ pound cheddar cheese
¶ ¼ cup sunflower seeds (optional)

Combine all ingredients, except cheese, milk powder, and seeds, with oil and 3 cups of water. Bring to boil and simmer for 15 minutes. Meanwhile, mix milk powder and remaining 1 cup water. Combine the two when polenta is cooked. Grate in cheddar cheese or cut in small chunks and stir in. Sprinkle with sunflower seeds if desired.

ONE-POT BROWN RICE AND SHRIMP

¶ serves two to three

¶ 2 cups brown rice
¶ 1 6½-ounce can shrimp or ½ cup freeze-dried shrimp
¶ large handful freeze-dried string beans
¶ 1 tablespoon onion flakes
¶ ½ teaspoon salt
¶ ⅛ teaspoon oregano
¶ ⅛ teaspoon thyme
¶ 1 tablespoon oil
¶ 5 cups water

To boiling water and oil add rice, salt, and onion. High simmer for 30 to 45 minutes. During the last few minutes add string beans and shrimp.

VARIATION: dried shrimp and dehydrated string beans may be used instead—add them halfway through cooking.

LENTIL TOMATO SOUP

¶ serves two

- ¶ ⅔ cup lentils
- ¶ ½ cup noodles, whole wheat, soy-rice, or sesame
- ¶ ¼ cup freeze-dried tomato powder
- ¶ 1 tablespoon vegetable-seasoned broth powder
- ¶ 2 teaspoons parsley flakes
- ¶ 1 teaspoon salt
- ¶ ¼ teaspoon garlic granules
- ¶ dash pepper
- ¶ 1 tablespoon oil
- ¶ 5 cups water

Add all ingredients to boiling water and oil and cook at a low boil for 30 to 40 minutes.

BARLEY SPLIT PEA SOUP

¶ serves three to four

¶ ¾ cup green split peas
¶ ½ cup barley
¶ 2 tablespoons dehydrated carrots
¶ 1 tablespoon celery flakes
¶ 2 teaspoons vegetable-seasoned broth powder
¶ 2 teaspoons onion flakes
¶ 1 teaspoon salt
¶ 1 teaspoon parsley flakes
¶ ⅛ teaspoon garlic granules
¶ 1 bay leaf
¶ 1 tablespoon oil
¶ 5 cups water

Bring water and oil to a boil. Slowly sprinkle in
dry ingredients. Stir; cover. Bring to boil again,
and keep at high simmer for 45 to 60 minutes or
until peas have softened.

ALPINE SPAGHETTI

A supper we had once in France and couldn't resist bringing home to the Sierra. Serve with salad of wild greens and maybe a little zinfandel.

¶ 8 ounces spaghetti or noodles
¶ 1 tablespoon olive oil
¶ 1 cup Parmesan cheese
¶ 3 teaspoons ground sweet basil
¶ 1 tablespoon parsley flakes
¶ 1 garlic clove, minced, or ⅛ teaspoon garlic
    granules
¶ water

Bring a pot of water to boil and add spaghetti. Boil for 10 minutes and drain. Add olive oil, toss, then add rest of ingredients and toss again until thoroughly mixed.

SPAGHETTI WITH GREENS

¶ serves two

This is a delicate spaghetti supper served hot, and it may also be eaten cold as a salad.

¶ 8 ounces spaghetti
¶ 1 tablespoon olive oil
¶ 1 tablespoon parsley flakes
¶ 1 teaspoon celery seed
¶ ¼ teaspoon salt
¶ ⅛ teaspoon pepper
¶ large handful or more of greens: sorrel, miners lettuce, dandelion greens, watercress
¶ water

Cook spaghetti in water with a little salt and oil. Drain off water, add cold water to cover, and drain again. In frying pan, heat up olive oil and rest of seasonings. Stir until hot, and add greens. Stir again, put on a lower fire and add a tablespoonful or so of water and cover. Let sit only 3 to 5 minutes, or until greens just begin to wilt. Combine the spaghetti and greens and toss well.

ANCHOVY SPAGHETTI

¶ serves two

¶ 8 ounces spaghetti, cooked in water with a
little salt and oil
¶ 1 2-ounce can anchovies and its oil
¶ 2 large cloves garlic, chopped fine
¶ handful greens

Drain hot water from spaghetti. In the meantime
pour anchovy oil into frying pan, add the garlic
and stir well until garlic begins to sizzle. Add the
anchovies, which have been cut into very small
pieces. Stir well and add the greens, which have
been broken into bite-size sections. Stir again and
cover. Let greens steam for only a few minutes.
Combine with the spaghetti, stirring greens
throughout the noodles. Serve hot or cold.

CORN CHOWDER
[CRAB OPTIONAL]

¶ serves two

A thick, creamy chowder, high in protein and a special treat with added crab.

¶ ½ cup dehydrated corn
¶ ½ cup freeze-dried potatoes or 1 raw unpeeled potato, cut in small pieces
¶ 2 tablespoons corn meal
¶ 2 tablespoons whole wheat flour
¶ 2 tablespoons soy milk powder
¶ 1 teaspoon parsley flakes
¶ 1 teaspoon onion flakes
¶ 1 teaspoon celery flakes
¶ ½ teaspoon salt
¶ ⅛ teaspoon paprika
¶ dash pepper
¶ 1 tablespoon butter
¶ 1 6½-ounce can cracked crab and juice (optional)
¶ 4¼ cups water

Combine all dry ingredients in one bag before you go. In camp combine all ingredients, except crab, in cold water and stir well. Bring to boil, stirring occasionally. Simmer for 10 to 15 minutes. Add can of crab and its juice, if desired, and heat through. Serve hot.

LENTIL NOODLE SOUP

- ¶ ¾ cup lentils
- ¶ ½ cup noodles, whole wheat, soy, or sesame
- ¶ 2 tablespoons whole wheat flour
- ¶ 2 teaspoons onion flakes
- ¶ ¾ teaspoon salt
- ¶ 1 bay leaf
- ¶ ⅛ teaspoon cloves, ground
- ¶ dash pepper
- ¶ 1 tablespoon apple cider vinegar *or* lemon juice
- ¶ 2 tablespoons oil
- ¶ 4 cups water

Add all ingredients to cold water, stir well, and bring to a boil. Simmer 30 to 40 minutes.

RICE CURRY

A special meal served with chapatis and chamomile tea.

¶ 1 cup rice
¶ 1 chopped onion or 1 tablespoon onion flakes
¶ 2 teaspoons curry powder
¶ ½ teaspoon salt
¶ 1 tablespoon oil
¶ 3 cups water
¶ handful of each: dried apricots, raisins, dates, chopped pears
¶ handful whole or chopped almonds, cashews or peanuts

Heat oil. Add rice, onion, and curry powder. Sauté for a few minutes. Add water, cover, and simmer for 30 minutes. Add dried fruit and nuts, cover again, and simmer 10 minutes more. Remove from heat and let sit covered 5 minutes.

GARNISHES: coconut, salted peanuts, wild onions, sliced fine.

VARIATION: use bulgar or millet, do not sauté.

CORN BEAN MUSH

¶ serves two to three

A thick mush, very good for supper with Garlic Bread or Cheese Toasties.

¶ ¾ cup cracked kidney beans (grind coarsely in loosely set grain grinder)
¶ ¼ cup dehydrated corn
¶ ¼ cup corn meal
¶ ¼ cup soy grits
¶ 3 tablespoons tomato powder
¶ 1 teaspoon onion flakes
¶ 1 teaspoon chili powder
¶ ¾ teaspoon salt
¶ ¼ teaspoon basil
¶ ¼ teaspoon oregano
¶ ⅛ teaspoon garlic granules
¶ dash cayenne
¶ ⅓ cup Parmesan cheese, grated
¶ 1 teaspoon corn oil
¶ 4 cups water

All dry ingredients (except cheese) may be combined in one bag. Add to pot with cold water and oil and bring to a boil, stirring often. Place on low fire and simmer for 30 minutes, stirring from time to time. When done, remove from heat and stir in Parmesan cheese. Serve hot.

FONDUE

A romantic supper for full-moon nuts.

¶ 1 pound Swiss cheese, grated
¶ 2 tablespoons whole wheat flour
¶ 1 garlic clove
¶ 2 cups dry white wine
¶ 1 loaf sourdough bread, broken into pieces

Rub pot with garlic and leave it in the pot. Pour in the wine and bring it to simmer. Mix cheese and flour, then stir in mixture and continue to stir until thick, about 10 minutes. Dip the pieces of broken bread in the fondue. Chopsticks are a good tool for this.

PINTO BEANS

- ¶ 1 cup pinto beans, cracked in a loose-set grain grinder
- ¶ 1 teaspoon cumin
- ¶ ½ teaspoon salt
- ¶ 1 garlic clove, minced
- ¶ pinch cayenne
- ¶ 1 tablespoon oil
- ¶ 4 cups water

Beans should be cracked about the size of split peas. Add all ingredients to boiling water and oil and simmer 30 minutes. Serve with Corn Pancakes and cheese.

VARIATION: add 1 teaspoon chili powder.

SPINACH CHEESE CASSEROLE

¶ serves two

- ¶ 1¼ cups brown rice
- ¶ ½ cup dehydrated spinach flakes
- ¶ ¼ cup dried mushrooms, sliced thin, chopped fine
- ¶ 1 minced garlic clove or ⅛ teaspoon garlic granules
- ¶ ½ teaspoon salt
- ¶ handful dried shrimp, 1 6½-ounce can, or ½ cup freeze-dried shrimp
- ¶ ½ pound raw milk cheddar cheese, grated or chopped in small chunks
- ¶ 1 teaspoon oil
- ¶ 3 cups water

Combine all ingredients except cheese and shrimp, if you used canned or freeze-dried. Bring to boil and simmer 45 to 60 minutes. Stir in cheese and canned or freeze-dried shrimp (unless you used dried). Cover for 2 to 3 minutes, then serve hot.

MUNG BEAN STEW

¶ serves two

If you haven't ever cooked mung beans as a bean
rather than as a sprout, you're in for a delicious
surprise. Their flavor somewhat resembles
black-eye peas, and they're good just plain with
soy sauce. This recipe makes a very thick
souplike broth with the beans for texture and the
sesames for crunch. Good on a chilly night.

¶   ½   cup mung beans
¶   ¼   cup corn meal
¶   ¼   cup toasted sesame seeds
¶   1   teaspoon onion flakes
¶   1   teaspoon parsley flakes
¶   ½   teaspoon salt
¶   ¼   pound cheddar cheese
¶   3½ cups water

All dry ingredients may be combined in one bag
beforehand. In camp, pour them all into cold
water. Bring to a boil, stirring occasionally.
Simmer for 30 minutes, remembering to stir from
time to time. Remove from heat. Cut cheese in
chunks (approximately ½ inch square) and add to
stew. Cover, let sit for 5 minutes, and serve hot.

CORN MEAL SPLIT PEA SOUP

¶ serves two

A hearty soup, well worth the wait.

¶ ½ cup split peas
¶ ½ cup corn meal
¶ 1 onion, chopped, or 1 tablespoon onion flakes
¶ 1 tablespoon celery flakes
¶ 1 tablespoon parsley flakes
¶ 1 garlic clove or ⅛ teaspoon garlic granules
¶ 1 bay leaf
¶ 1 teaspoon cumin
¶ ½ teaspoon savory
¶ ½ teaspoon salt
¶ ⅛ teaspoon cayenne
¶ 2 tablespoons olive oil
¶ 1 tablespoon tamari soy sauce
¶ 4 cups water

Bring ingredients to simmer over low heat, stirring occasionally. Cook 45 to 60 minutes.

ASIAN RICE AND LENTILS

¶ serves two

Rice and lentils, when eaten together, make a richer balance of protein than if they are eaten separately.

¶ ½ cup brown rice
¶ ½ cup lentils
¶ 2 tablespoons butter
¶ 1 onion, chopped, or 1 tablespoon onion flakes
¶ ½ teaspoon salt
¶ ½ teaspoon cinnamon
¶ ½ teaspoon ginger
¶ ½ teaspoon cardamon
¶ 2 whole cloves
¶ 1 bay leaf
¶ pinch cayenne (optional)
¶ 2½ cups water

Melt butter in cook-pot and add all dry ingredients. Sauté a few minutes and then cover with water. Cover pot, place over low heat, and cook 45 to 60 minutes. To reduce cooking time in camp, try cracking rice and lentils in loosely set grain grinder at home.

GREEN NOODLE SALAD

¶ serves two

It's a good idea to make this when you have your breakfast fire going, and let sit in the pot until lunch or supper, at which time you may add some foraged greens. It's filling, and would be very good for a supper dish, to be eaten while you wait for the soup to cook.

¶ 8   ounces green or mixed vegetable noodles
¶ ¼   cup parsley flakes
¶ 2   tablespoons onion flakes
¶ 1   teaspoon salt
¶ ½   teaspoon basil
¶ ¼   teaspoon oregano
¶ ¼   teaspoon garlic granules
¶ 1   tablespoon olive oil
¶ lemon juice *or* apple cider vinegar
¶ 2½ cups water

Bring water and oil to a boil, and add all dry ingredients. Boil slowly for 10 minutes or until noodles are done. Let cool from 1 hour to all day. When ready to eat, toss in vinegar or lemon juice and any found greens, which have been broken into bite-sized pieces.

SAUCES AND GRAVIES

We feel that sauces and gravies are a very important part of backpacking food. They turn plain noodles, grains, or patties into something special. Nourishing and inexpensive, they add variety in taste, are simple to make and are warming on cold days.

SEAFOOD CURRY SAUCE

This turns out thick like chowder and, served with chapatis and wild greens, it makes a delicious meal. Easy and quick to make, even in your tent on a snowy eve. It's good served over noodles and grains, too.

- ¶ ¼ cup tomato powder
- ¶ 5 teaspoons curry powder
- ¶ 1 tablespoon parsley flakes
- ¶ ½ teaspoon cumin, ground
- ¶ ½ teaspoon coriander seed, ground
- ¶ ½ teaspoon ginger
- ¶ ½ teaspoon salt
- ¶ ½ teaspoon tarragon (optional)
- ¶ 1 onion, chopped, or 1 tablespoon onion flakes
- ¶ 1 clove garlic, minced, or ⅛ teaspoon garlic granules
- ¶ 2 teaspoons tamari soy sauce
- ¶ 2 cups water
- ¶ 1 6½-ounce can shrimp, tuna, or other seafood or ½ cup freeze-dried seafood

Mix all ingredients except seafood. (If using fresh onion, sauté it first.) Simmer 5 to 10 minutes. Add seafood and let sit 1 minute.

CHEESE SAUCE

¶ approximately 2 cups

Very quick, very creamy.

¶ ½ cup milk powder
¶ 2 tablespoons whole wheat flour
¶ 1 teaspoon parsley flakes
¶ ½ teaspoon salt
¶ ¼ teaspoon dry mustard
¶ dash cayenne
¶ 1¾ cups water
¶ ¼ pound grated Monterey Jack or your favorite mild cheese

Mix water with dry ingredients. Bring just to bubbling point, stirring all the while. Remove from heat, add cheese, stir well, and serve. Soya-bacon bits are a tasty addition as a garnish when serving this over noodles.

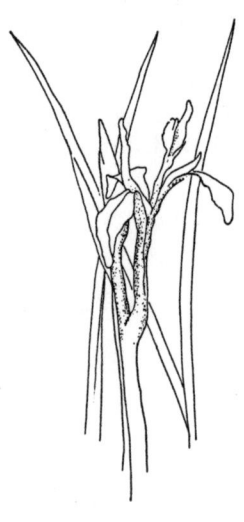

TUNA SAUCE

¶ approximately 2½ cups

This recipe is for one of those nights when you counted on fresh fish all day, but for some reason they just weren't biting.

- ¶ 1 6½-ounce can tuna and its oil
- ¶ ¼ cup milk powder
- ¶ 2 tablespoons whole wheat flour
- ¶ 1 tablespoon parsley flakes
- ¶ ¼ teaspoon salt
- ¶ ⅛ teaspoon dill weed
- ¶ dash cayenne or black pepper
- ¶ 1 cup water

Drain oil from tuna into cold frying pan (should equal 2 tablespoons). Add dry ingredients and mix well. Stir water in slowly and bring to a boil. Add tuna and stir until thick. Serve hot over grains, noodles, patties, or even broken pieces of bread or toast. This recipe can serve four with one can of tuna by doubling everything else.

TOMATO SAUCE

¶ 3½ to 4 cups

This is our spaghetti sauce and we also use it over grains and patties. Tastes like fresh homemade.

- ¶ ½ cup tomato powder
- ¶ ¼ cup dried mushrooms, sliced thin and chopped fine, or 1 cup fresh wild mushrooms, chopped (optional)
- ¶ ¼ cup dehydrated bell pepper (optional)
- ¶ 3 tablespoons tomato flakes (optional)
- ¶ 1 fresh onion, chopped, or wild green onions, sliced, or 2 tablespoons onion flakes
- ¶ 1 tablespoon parsley flakes
- ¶ 1 teaspoon oregano
- ¶ 1 teaspoon basil
- ¶ ½ teaspoon salt
- ¶ 1 garlic clove, minced, or ⅛ teaspoon garlic granules
- ¶ 1 6½-ounce can crab, clams, or shrimp or ½ cup freeze-dried shrimp (optional)
- ¶ 1 tablespoon oil
- ¶ 3 cups water

Bring water and oil to a boil and add all ingredients except seafood. Cook for 25 minutes. Add seafood and heat through. Garnish with Parmesan cheese.

VARIATIONS: 1 small can bonita or mackerel or 1 cup freshly cooked flaked fish may be used instead of seafood.

One-Pot Spaghetti: simply add 1 cup extra water to sauce and drop in noodles when sauce comes to a boil.

CHILI SAUCE

¶ approximately 3½ cups

Serve over grains, noodles, polenta, or journey cakes.

¶ ¼ cup tomato powder
¶ 1 small onion, chopped, or wild onions, sliced, or 1 tablespoon onion flakes
¶ 1 tablespoon whole wheat flour, masa, or corn flour
¶ 1 teaspoon chili powder
¶ 1 teaspoon cumin, ground
¶ 1 teaspoon oregano, rubbed between the palms of your hands
¶ 1 teaspoon parsley flakes
¶ ½ teaspoon salt
¶ 1 garlic clove, minced, or ⅛ teaspoon garlic granules
¶ 1 tablespoon olive oil
¶ 3 cups water
¶ 1 6½-ounce can shrimp or ½ cup freeze-dried shrimp (optional)

Combine everything but the shrimp. Bring to simmer over low heat and cook 5 to 10 minutes. Add shrimp and heat through.

VARIATION: add fresh chopped wild mushrooms.

WHOLE WHEAT GRAVY

¶ approximately 2 cups

- ¶ ½ cup whole wheat flour
- ¶ 1 teaspoon parsley flakes
- ¶ 1 teaspoon onion flakes
- ¶ ½ teaspoon salt
- ¶ 1 bay leaf *or* ¼ teaspoon either sage, thyme, marjoram, or oregano
- ¶ ⅛ teaspoon garlic granules
- ¶ 1 tablespoon oil
- ¶ 2 cups water
- ¶ 2 teaspoons tamari soy sauce

Mix oil and dry ingredients in frying pan and slowly add cold water. Place over medium hot heat and cook until thick, stirring all the while, about 5 to 10 minutes. Add tamari and serve hot.

MISO GRAVY

¶ approximately 1½ cups

- ¶ 1 small onion, sliced thin and chopped fine, or handful wild onions, sliced
- ¶ 2 tablespoons whole wheat flour
- ¶ ¼ teaspoon ginger powder *or* grated orange peel (optional)
- ¶ 1 teaspoon sesame oil
- ¶ 2 teaspoons miso
- ¶ 1 cup water

Heat oil; add onions and stir until they become a little transparent. Add flour and ginger and stir until onions are coated and flour starts to brown. Mix the miso into the water, and stir this into the other mixture. Lower heat and then cook only a minute or so longer.

MUSHROOM GRAVY

¶ 1 cup

A thick, rich gravy, strong in mushroom flavor.

¶ ¼ cup dried mushrooms, sliced thin, chopped fine
¶ 2 tablespoons whole wheat flour
¶ 2 tablespoons milk powder
¶ 1 tablespoon freeze-dried chopped chives
¶ 2 teaspoons vegetable-seasoned broth powder
¶ 1 teaspoon parsley flakes
¶ ¼ teaspoon salt
¶ ⅛ teaspoon garlic granules
¶ dash pepper
¶ 1 teaspoon oil or butter
¶ 1¼ cups water

Combine all dry ingredients at home in small packet. In camp, mix in cold water and stir well. Bring to a boil, then move to low fire, stir well, and cook for 5 minutes longer. Cover, remove from heat, and let sit for 5 minutes before serving.

CURRY GRAVY

¶ 1 cup

A gravy adds so much to a meal, making a small one complete.

¶ 2 tablespoons milk powder
¶ 2 tablespoons whole wheat flour
¶ 1 teaspoon onion flakes
¶ 1 teaspoon parsley flakes
¶ ¾ teaspoon curry powder
¶ ¼ teaspoon salt
¶ 1 cup water

All dry ingredients may be packed in one bag. In camp, pour into cold water and stir well. Bring to boil, reduce heat, stir well, and simmer for 5 minutes.

PEANUT BUTTER GRAVY

¶ approximately 1½ cups

¶ ½ cup peanut butter
¶ 1 tablespoon whole wheat flour
¶ pinch garlic granules
¶ dash cayenne
¶ 1 teaspoon tamari soy sauce
¶ 1 cup water

Combine all ingredients except water and tamari. Mix well; add water and heat, stirring continuously, until bubbly. Remove from heat, add tamari. Serve hot.

CASHEW GRAVY

¶ approximately 3 cups

A mild gravy, simple to make, that adds protein to the meal.

¶ ¾   cup cashews, ground fine
¶ 2   tablespoons arrowroot powder
¶ 1   teaspoon parsley flakes
¶ 1   teaspoon onion powder
¶ ½   teaspoon celery flakes
¶ ½   teaspoon salt
¶ ¼   teaspoon celery seed
¶ 2½ to 3 cups water

At home, grind cashews in blender or seed grinder. Bag with remaining dry ingredients. In camp, mix with water and stir over medium heat till thick. Serve hot.

GRAB BAG

Carry the staples in one bag and the seasonings in another.

This is a simple and more flexible way of packaging food for cooking along the trail. Package the staples for each basic recipe in bags, leaving the vegetables and seasonings to go in separate small bags or plastic bottles, combining and creating as you go along. This way a few basic ingredients can offer a surprising variety of meals, and suit the mood and ambition of the cook. The variations are so broad that not only can they be used in each different meal, but they can cover several days of food without repetition. Try Mountain Gruel with raisins and honey for breakfast, and for supper the same Mountain Gruel made up with onions, herbs and miso. The variations are endless—use your imagination and have fun. This way can also be of help when you are packing up in a hurry and want to plan your menu later.

MISO SOUP

¶ serves two

Miso should be in everybody's pack, along with a little seaweed and dried fish. It's worth its weight in gold. It can make a complete meal or could be a broth before a meal. It's a very good hot broth by itself for quick energy. Good for breakfast, too.

¶ 4 by 4-inch piece of kombu (seaweed)
¶ 3 tablespoons dried fish flakes *or* handful iriki (small dried fish)
¶ 2 tablespoons miso
¶ 2 teaspoons tamari soy sauce
¶ 1 teaspoon oil
¶ 4 cups water

Combine water, kombu, and fish flakes. Bring to a boil and let boil for 5 minutes. Remove from heat and let sit for 3 minutes. Return to heat. Stir in miso or strain in, if desired, until all is dissolved into the soup. Add tamari and serve.

VARIATIONS: add 8 ounces noodles at the beginning; drop in Fish Dumplings at the beginning and cook 10 minutes in all; add any wild greens when finished, cover, and let sit for 5 minutes before serving; add dried shrimp at the beginning or canned fish or shrimp at the end; see Seaweed Soup and Watercress Soup.

GARNISHES: chopped mountain sorrel, watercress, miners lettuce, borage; sliced lemon; wild onions, sliced very fine; broken pieces of zwieback; popcorn; dried chives; Parmesan cheese.

GARLIC BROTH

¶ 1 quart

A basic and nourishing broth, it is easy and cheap to make. It's fine the way it is or with a little Parmesan cheese sprinkled on top. A good base for soup or stew. Try it with a fresh potato cooked in it. Or rice, lentils, wild greens, barley, croutons. . . .

¶   16 to 20 garlic cloves
¶   1 tablespoon parsley flakes
¶   ¼ teaspoon sage
¶   ¼ teaspoon thyme
¶   1 clove
¶   1 small bay leaf
¶   2 tablespoons olive oil
¶   1 quart water

Combine all ingredients and simmer 30 minutes.

POLENTA MUSH

Polenta is a special grind of corn that can be found in any store carrying Italian foods. If you can't find polenta, corn meal will do just fine. It cooks up thick and can be sweet or savory depending on what you add. It is good plain as a cereal with dried fruit or made into cakes and served with cheese and tomato sauce. A good staple for the pack.

BASIC RECIPE

¶ 1 cup polenta or corn meal
¶ 2 tablespoons soy grits (optional)
¶ 1 teaspoon salt
¶ 6 cups water

Mix ingredients and bring to simmer. Cook 5 to 10 minutes. Try substituting brown rice flour, barley flour, or millet flour for some of the polenta.

FOR CEREAL, add to Basic Recipe any of the following:

¶ dry fruit
¶ nuts
¶ seeds
¶ nut or seed butters
¶ milk powder
¶ butter
¶ honey
¶ maple syrup
¶ tamari soy sauce

Cook as above, adding ingredients to your taste.

For ONE-POT MEAL, add to the Basic Recipe one of the following combinations:

¶ wild greens, onion, garlic, nuts, seeds, parsley flakes, rosemary, thyme
¶ tuna or shrimp with onion, garlic, and dill
¶ walnuts and cheddar cheese
¶ cheese, freeze-dried or dehydrated vegetables, oregano, marjoram, basil, bay leaf, thyme, onions
¶ freeze-dried beans, chili powder, oregano, cumin, onions, garlic
¶ chunks of cheese, Tomato Sauce

Cook any combinations you choose for 5 to 10 minutes, saving the cheese for last.

For FRIED MUSH CAKES, form leftovers into patties and fry in a little butter. Serve cold as a bread with peanut butter or hot with Chili Sauce and cheese.

This mush is at its finest when cooked plain, allowed to cool, sliced, fried, and served in a bowl with sliced cheese and then Tomato Sauce, perhaps with cooked mung beans in it, poured over the top.

Plain mush cakes are good fried for breakfast and eaten with maple or Honey Syrup.

MOUNTAIN GRUEL

A basic recipe with many options: soup, cereal, one-pot meal, pudding, or patties.

BASIC RECIPE

¶ ½ cup rolled oats
¶ ½ cup rolled wheat
¶ 2 tablespoons soy grits
¶ 2 to 4 cups water
¶ 1 tablespoon oil or butter (optional)

Combine ingredients and simmer 10 to 15 minutes, stirring occasionally. Try using rolled rye, corn, barley, or other grains instead of oats or wheat.

FOR CEREAL #1, add to Basic Recipe any or all of the following to taste:

¶ raisins or other dried fruit
¶ nuts or seeds
¶ wheat germ flakes
¶ milk powder
¶ cinnamon
¶ honey

Combine ingredients in 2 cups water, saving milk powder for the last few minutes. Cook over low heat for 10 minutes.

FOR CEREAL #2, toast Basic Recipe first, and then add 2 cups water and cook for 10 minutes over low fire. Season with soy sauce or sesame salt. A few raisins make a good addition.

For dessert, follow Cereal #1, adding:

¶ vanilla
¶ more milk powder
¶ allspice, cloves, nutmeg, and/or ginger
¶ substitute molasses or maple syrup for honey

For soup, follow Basic Recipe and season with any of the following combinations, according to taste:

¶ onion, garlic, wild greens, parsley, bay leaf
¶ tomato powder, miso, cumin, oregano
¶ raisins, apricots, curry powder, ginger, coriander
¶ vegetable-seasoned broth powder, dehydrated or freeze-dried vegetables, thyme, marjoram, sage, tamari soy sauce
¶ cheese, milk powder, sweet basil

Combine desired ingredients with 4 cups water, 1 teaspoon salt, and Basic Recipe. Cook over low heat for 10 to 15 minutes. When using cheese or milk, stir them in during last few minutes.

For one-pot meals, add to the Basic Recipe one of the following combinations:

¶ lentils (precooked for 30 minutes), miso, onions, garlic, parsley, thyme, bay leaf, sage, tomato powder
¶ noodles, nuts, seeds, savory, chervil, cheese
¶ millet (precooked for 30 minutes), Parmesan cheese, fish or shrimp

Combine desired ingredients with 3 cups water, 1 teaspoon salt, and Basic Recipe. Cook over low heat for 10 to 15 minutes. Stir in cheese at the end, just before serving.

For patties, use leftover One-Pot Meal, or make a thicker One-Pot Meal recipe and form into patties and fry. Serve with a sauce or gravy.

DOUG'S BULGAR

Bulgar is precooked cracked wheat, so it makes a quick-cooking dinner base for building seafood variations.

¶ 1 cup bulgar
¶ 2 tablespoons soy grits
¶ 2 to 4 cups water depending on how thick you like your stew or what else you are adding
¶ 1 tablespoon vegetable broth powder
¶ 1 tablespoon oil
¶ 1 or 2 cloves garlic
¶ ½ teaspoon salt
¶ 1 or 2 bay leaves

Combine first 3 ingredients, and put on to simmer. Stir in remaining ingredients and continue to simmer about 15 minutes.

VARIATIONS: add small handfuls of your favorite dried vegetables: onion, parsley, mushrooms, tomato flakes, celery. Try a fresh onion for a treat. Or add: oregano, basil, thyme, sage, tamari soy sauce. Add just before serving: albacore, salmon, mackerel, freeze-dried shrimp or crab.

FOR BREAKFAST, add butter and honey, dried fruit and nuts.

MACARONI AND CHEESE

BASIC RECIPE

¶ 2 to 3 cups water
¶ 1 cup macaroni (wheat, buckwheat, soy)
¶ ¼ pound cheese (cheddar, Swiss, Jack)
¶ ¼ cup milk powder
¶ 1 tablespoon parsley flakes
¶ 1 garlic clove, minced, or ⅛ teaspoon garlic
 granules

Bring salted water to a boil. Add macaroni and cook till done, about 10 minutes. Drain. Add remaining ingredients. Stir over low heat until cheese is melted.

VARIATIONS: add canned tuna or shrimp; add chopped onion along with macaroni, omit draining; add a little chili powder and ground cumin; use buckwheat noodles and season with oregano; season with rosemary, basil, or savory; omit garlic and add chopped walnuts.

DESSERTS

Children and celebrations. A
surprise birthday cake, snow ice
cream, or sweetness after
a light supper.

CREAMY TAPIOCA PUDDING

¶ serves two

- ¶ ⅔ cup milk powder
- ¶ 3 tablespoons tapioca
- ¶ pinch salt
- ¶ 1 tablespoon honey
- ¶ 2 cups water
- ¶ 1 teaspoon vanilla

Combine all ingredients except vanilla. Bring to simmer and cook till thick, stirring constantly. Stir in vanilla and serve hot.

VARIATION: for carob pudding, add 2 tablespoons carob powder.

TAPIOCA FRUIT PUDDING

¶ serves two

Like Stewed Fruit, but with a texture and flavor all its own.

- ¶ 2 cups mixed dried fruit and nuts
- ¶ 3 tablespoons tapioca granules
- ¶ 1 tablespoon rose hip powder
- ¶ 1 tablespoon honey
- ¶ juice of 1 lemon or lime
- ¶ 2½ cups water

Combine ingredients in cold water. Bring to simmer and cook 5 to 10 minutes or until thick, stirring often. Serve warm or cold.

APPLE BARLEY PUDDING

¶ serves four

A good dessert after a light supper.

¶ 1 cup rolled barley
¶ 1 cup Home-Dried Apples,
    chopped
¶ ½ cup raisins
¶ handful nuts
¶ 1 teaspoon cinnamon
¶ ½ teaspoon nutmeg
¶ dash cloves (optional)
¶ 3 cups water
¶ honey to taste

Combine ingredients, reserving honey until pudding is cooked. Simmer 5 to 10 minutes, add honey and stir. Serve hot.

APPLE SAUCE

¶ serves two

¶ 2 cups Home-Dried Apples,
    chopped and pressed gently down into
      measuring cup
¶ water
¶ 1 tablespoon honey

Add enough water to just barely cover apples. Simmer until soft and saucey. Add honey. Serve warm or cold.

VARIATIONS: add ½ teaspoon cinnamon, squeeze of lemon, raisins, nuts.

APPLE CRISP

A surprisingly delicious and easy to make dessert. Everybody loves it.

¶ ¼   pound Home-Dried Apples
¶ 1½ to 2 cups water
¶ ½   teaspoon cinnamon
¶ big pinch nutmeg
¶ squeeze lemon
¶ 1   cup rolled oats
¶ ¼   cup whole wheat flour
¶ 2   tablespoons oil
¶ 2   teaspoons honey
¶ ¼   teaspoon salt

Soak apples in water for 10 minutes. Place in buttered frying pan and sprinkle on cinnamon, nutmeg, and lemon juice. Meanwhile, mix up remaining ingredients and sprinkle over apple mixture. Cover and bake in coals 15 to 20 minutes.

HIGH MOUNTAIN PIE

¶ serves four to six

A favorite of ours. May be baked as a cake or served like shortcake.

¶ 2 cups mixed dried fruit—apricots, apples, figs, prunes, raisins, pears, pineapple, dates
¶ large handful walnuts or pecans
¶ 1 tablespoon honey
¶ 1 teaspoon cinnamon

Cover fruit with water and stew 10 minutes. Add honey, cinnamon and nuts and pour into buttered fry pan. Cover with the following batter:

¶ 1 cup brown rice flour
¶ ¼ cup wheat germ flakes
¶ 2 tablespoons milk powder
¶ 1 teaspoon baking powder
¶ 2 tablespoons honey
¶ 1 tablespoon oil
¶ ½ cup water

Mix ingredients together and pour over fruit mixture. Cover frying pan and place in low-burning coals. Bake for 30 minutes or until crust is golden brown and springy to the touch.

VARIATION: if coal baking is inconvenient, or you want this quickly, cook fruit as usual and bake topping in small pancakes, making the batter thinner. Pour fruit over cakes and serve hot.

PINEAPPLE UPSIDE DOWN CAKE

¶ serves four to six

Who would have ever guessed it.

¶ 1 cup whole wheat flour
¶ ¾ cup rice flour
¶ ½ cup soy milk powder
¶ ½ cup wheat germ flakes
¶ 2 teaspoons baking powder
¶ ½ teaspoon salt
¶ ½ cup honey
¶ ¼ cup oil
¶ 2 teaspoons vanilla
¶ 1 cup water
¶ 1 to 1½ cups dried pineapple pieces
¶ 1 cup walnuts or pecan pieces
¶ butter

Combine flour, milk powder, wheat germ flakes, baking powder, and salt with ⅓ cup honey, oil, water, and vanilla. Dot frying pan with butter and sprinkle on nuts, pineapple pieces, and remaining honey to taste. Pour on batter, cover pan, and place in low-burning coals. Bake approximately 30 minutes. Baking can also be done in a well-sealed pan on the grate over a slow fire.

WALNUT RAISIN SPICE CAKE

Honey and spice and everything nice.

- ¶ 1¼ cups whole wheat flour
- ¶ ½ cup oat flour
- ¶ ½ cup rice flour
- ¶ ½ cup wheat germ flakes
- ¶ ½ cup soy milk powder
- ¶ 2 teaspoons baking powder
- ¶ 1 teaspoon cinnamon
- ¶ ½ teaspoon cloves
- ¶ ½ teaspoon nutmeg
- ¶ ½ teaspoon salt
- ¶ handful each walnuts, raisins, and chopped dried apples
- ¶ ½ cup honey
- ¶ ¼ cup oil
- ¶ 2 teaspoons vanilla
- ¶ 1 cup water

Combine dry ingredients with liquids. Stir well and pour into oiled frying pan. Cover, nestle pan in coals, bake 30 to 40 minutes until springy.

FROSTINGS

¶ enough for one 6" frying pan cake

Basic Vanilla Frosting:

- ¶ 2 tablespoons honey
- ¶ 1 to 1½ tablespoons butter
- ¶ ½ teaspoon vanilla

Crunchy Frosting:

(add to above)
- ¶ 1 teaspoon date sugar

Spice Frosting:

(add to Basic Vanilla Frosting)
- ¶ 1 teaspoon date sugar (optional)
- ¶ ⅛ teaspoon cinnamon
- ¶ dash cloves, nutmeg

Carob Frosting:

(add to Basic Vanilla Frosting)
- ¶ 3 tablespoons carob powder

DATE WALNUT TOPPING [hot or cold]

¶ approximately ¾ cup

Serve for a sweet topping on Meal Cakes, bread, or pancakes.

- ¶ ½ cup dates, pitted and sliced
- ¶ ¼ cup walnuts, chopped fine
- ¶ ½ cup water

Place in small pan on heat. Stir until warmed through.

SNOW ICE CREAM

A delicious refresher—especially suited for ski-touring trips and sweet moments.

Fill cup with fresh clean snow. Pour over snow:

¶ apple or orange juice concentrate (may be bought in small cans)
¶ any berry concentrate (in small bottles) diluted in advance with half water
¶ maple syrup
¶ Honey Syrup

Eat/drink with or without a spoon.

snowberries, huckleberries, bunchberries, chokecherries, serviceberries, winterberries, gooseberries, currants, salal, loganberries, barberries, elderberries, thimbleberries, blackberries, strawberries, raspberries, blueberries.

BEVERAGES

It is important to remember to get enough liquids while on the trail, as the extra energy used, the climate change, and the altitude change cause dehydration, and it happens before you know it.

Mountain streams offer the best pure drink available, and we suggest that you stop often for some of this fresh cold water (it's wisest to choose water that bubbles a lot, moves fast, and gets sunshine), following precautions described in the Hints section of this book.

HERBAL TONIC TEAS

Tonics are herbs that have a generally invigorating and stimulating effect on the system, toning muscles and organs. You should try some of these tonic teas and become familiar with tastes and effects that suit you and your family and friends. We encourage you to take the time to discover and learn about some of these beneficial plants. You will be surprised at how easy it is to learn to recognize herbs growing along the trail and on your hikes. In a short time, with a little practice, you will be able to discover for yourself the satisfaction of recognizing, collecting, and using many of them.

Here is a general list of tonic teas that may be easily purchased dried at natural food stores, and many of which you will find along the trail:

catnip leaves	parsley leaves and root
celery seeds	peppermint leaves
chamomile flower tips	raspberry leaves
comfrey leaves	red clover flower tips
ginseng root	rose hips
golden seal root	sage leaves
juniper berries	sassafras bark
mugwort, whole plant	thyme leaves
nettle flowers,	yarrow, whole plant
leaves and seeds	yellow dock root
orange and lemon rinds	yerba santa leaves

The standard amount of herbs to use is 1 teaspoon per cup of water. In general, if you are using leaves and delicate parts of plants, merely pour boiling water over them, steep for 5 to 10 minutes, strain, and serve. If you are dealing with the roots or bark, add them to the pot of boiling water, lower heat, and low boil from 15 to 30 minutes. Combinations of teas are a good idea, and you will soon find combinations that suit your needs. Usually we combine two or three, but certainly more may be used. Also, it would be a good idea to switch these herbs from time to time, so your system doesn't get saturated with any particular one. Dried tea leaves are very lightweight and the most rewarding drink we can recommend aside from pure water. Honey may be added to any of these tonic teas.

SUN-INFUSED HERBAL TEA

¶ 1 quart

Early in the morning, as soon as you feel the sun beginning to warm your body, collect 4 cups of fresh water in a quart bottle with a lid. Add 4 teaspoons dried herbs or a handful of fresh, if you are so lucky to find some, and set jar in the sun on a rock. Let sit until the sun starts to go down, then strain and serve. You might want to put the jar in a creek to cool it even more before straining.

SUN-INFUSED HERBAL LEMONADE

¶ 1 quart

A luxury for the little ones who might be accompanying you on your journey. Follow directions for Herbal Tea, except add 4 tablespoons lemon juice and 2 tablespoons honey when you add the herbs. Especially good for children are peppermint, chamomile, catnip, alfalfa, red clover, hyssop, and comfrey. These may be used individually or in combinations of two or three. A sunshine-sweet drink!

LEMONADE

¶ 1 cup

Lemons are the best thirst quenchers. Take a few lemons for lemonade. One lemon in a gallon of water will keep the water fresh if you have to carry it for several days.

¶ 2 tablespoons lemon juice
¶ 2 teaspoons honey
¶ 1 cup water

Combine. You may have to use ¼ cup hot water first to dissolve honey and then add ¾ cup cold. For hot days, prepare in the morning, put in a jar with a lid, and place in edge of stream. If you are in cold weather, however, this is also very good heated.

LEMON WATER

Very refreshing, and feels good in your mouth. Try this recipe using lime, too.

Squeeze a half a lemon in your cup and fill it with cold water. Swish it around and drink. Better than powdered.

CAROB MILK [hot and cold]

¶ 1 quart

This milk drink is a healthy replacement for chocolate milk. It's high in calcium and food energy and builds the body rather than tearing it down. It's so pleasant to sit around the campfire sipping a cup of hot carob, watching the stars come out. . . .

¶ 1 cup milk powder
¶ ⅓ cup carob powder
¶ 1 tablespoon honey
¶ ½ teaspoon vanilla
¶ 4 cups water

COLD: put 3 cups cold water in your quart bottle. Add milk powder and carob. Screw lid on tight and shake well until all is mixed. Stir honey in a small container or cup with a little bit of warm water to dissolve it. Add honey and vanilla to drink and fill almost to top with cold water. Shake and serve.

HOT: combine all ingredients in saucepan. Heat, stirring frequently; do not boil. Serve when hot.

FRUIT JUICE CONCENTRATES

Most natural food stores have such a product available without added sugar (proportion of concentrate to water is usually 1 to 5, but some vary—it will say on bottle). They are a real treat and also help on winter expeditions to add a touch of fresh fruit flavor. To mention a few: red and black raspberry, blueberry, black currant, apricot, blackberry, peach, plum, grape, black cherry, cranberry, boysenberry.

We recommend rationing these drinks carefully, as the liquid concentrate adds up fast, weight-wise, and money-wise, but this is such a refreshing, sweet-tasting liquid, besides being a very good tonic drink, that we suggest you try a little bit for at least one hot afternoon. These drinks are also very good warm, for cold mornings and evenings. Children will love you for taking the trouble to pack it in.

ROSE HIP DRINK

¶ 3 cups

Very good on a cold winter night or early in the morning when your tent is still frost-covered; high in vitamin C.

¶ 2 tablespoons rose hip powder
¶ ¼ cup maple syrup
¶ 3 cups water

Combine, heat, and serve.

ANISE MILK DRINK
[hot and cold]

The delicate flavor of anise makes this sweet drink a favorite.

¶ 1¼ cups milk powder
¶ 1 teaspoon anise seeds
¶ 2 tablespoons honey
¶ 4 cups water
¶ butter, for hot drink

COLD: for a day when you are leaving a camp set up and may be going on a day hike away from camp, and you know you will want a good drink when you return. In plastic quart bottle, combine milk powder, honey, and anise in 2 to 3 cups water. Put on lid and shake well. Set bottle on a rock in a place where the sun will hit it all day. When you return to camp in the evening, fill rest of container full of water and shake. If it is still too warm, place bottle in a stream for a short while if possible. Strain and serve.

HOT: combine all ingredients in saucepan. Stir well and heat through until quite warm, but do not boil. Remove from heat, cover, and let sit for 5 minutes. Strain into cups and add a lump of butter in each cup. Children love it!

CASHEW MILK

¶ 2 cups

A delicious addition poured over hot cereal or pudding, millet and dates, rice and raisins. A refreshing drink for small children.

¶ 1 cup cashews, ground fine
¶ 1 tablespoon honey
¶ 1 teaspoon vanilla
¶ 2 cups water

At home, grind nuts and mix in vanilla and honey. Carry in plastic bottle. In camp or on the trail, slowly add cold fresh water and mix well.

VARIATION: for almond milk, follow recipe but blanch and peel almonds first.

ODDS AND ENDS

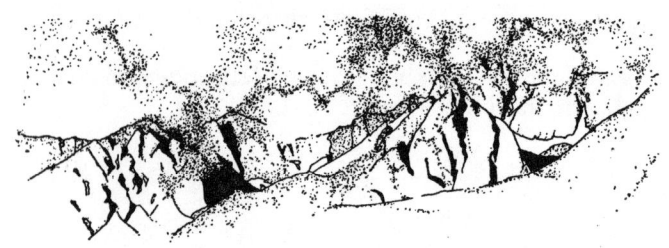

Stewed Fruit, Cheese Toasties,
Sesame Salt, Wakame, Cornbread,
and other miscellaneous recipes.
Enjoy yourself.

STEWED FRUIT

¶ approximately 2 to 3 cups

A light breakfast by itself, or with heated chapatis and peanut butter. Add some spice and serve for dessert, hot or cold.

Soak 2 cups of any combination of unsulphured dried fruit overnight with water to cover 1 inch above fruit. In the morning, simmer 5 to 10 minutes. Omit soaking if fruit is exceptionally soft.

Good over granola, pancakes, cornbread, grains, hot cereal, and Meal Cakes.

VARIATIONS: add lemon, orange, cinnamon, and/or cloves.

FOR DRIED FRUIT JAM: barely cover fruit with water and soak 10 minutes. Add 1 tablespoon honey per cup of fruit. Simmer till thick. Try apricots and dates together.

STEAMED GREENS

chicory, dandelion greens, sorrel, miners lettuce, chickweed, wild onions, and wild garlic

If you come upon a big patch of edible wild greens and a few handfuls won't be missed, you are in for a treat.

Fill a 2-quart cook-pot with washed greens, add about ½ inch of water, cover as tightly as possible (maybe a big rock will help), bring to a boil, and steam only 3 to 5 minutes. Serve with sesame seeds, soy sauce, grated cheese, cooked potato, mushrooms, salad dressing, cooked noodles, or vegetable broth (made in juice).

Remember, when picking greens, please never take more than you need or will use.

STIR FRY GREENS

In hot fry pan, put 1 teaspoon oil and add assorted greens. Stir fry for 3 minutes. Add:

¶ tamari soy sauce
¶ lemon juice
¶ sesame seeds

Cover and remove from heat. Let sit a couple of minutes and serve.

CORNBREAD

¶ serves four to six

Everybody likes cornbread, hot from the coals. Serve with maple syrup for breakfast, smothered in pinto beans for supper, dripping with butter and honey for dessert, or cold with peanut butter or cheese for lunch.

¶ 1½ cups corn meal
¶ ½ cup whole wheat flour
¶ ½ cup wheat germ flakes
¶ ½ cup soy milk powder
¶ 2 teaspoons baking powder
¶ 1 teaspoon salt
¶ ¼ cup oil
¶ 2 tablespoons honey
¶ 1½ cups water

Mix dry ingredients with liquids and stir well. Pour into oiled frying pan and cover. Nestle in soft coals (ones that have just turned gray), raking some up around the sides and over the top of pan. Let bread bake *slowly,* for 30 minutes.

VARIATIONS: add walnuts, chopped; poppy seeds; *or* sunflower seeds, chopped.

CHEESE TOASTIES

Take pieces of bread, journey cakes, crackers, pancakes, or leftover patties and put slices of cheese on them. (Butter bread first if desired.) Place in frying pan, cover, and put over slow fire. Toast until cheese melts. This also may be done on a flat rock next to coals. Serve with soup, stew, or wild greens salad.

GARLIC BREAD

Melt some butter in a pot and add a few sliced garlic cloves. Meanwhile, start toasting bread slices in frying pan or over fire. When one side is done, turn and spoon on garlic butter and continue toasting. Garlic granules may be used instead of fresh garlic.

POPPED SEEDS

Heat frying pan and add 1 cup, mixed or by themselves: hulled pumpkin seeds, sunflower seeds, squash seeds. Toast lightly, stirring all the while. When all seems to have popped or become brown, add 1 to 2 teaspoons soy sauce per cup of seeds and stir well and quickly, as the sauce crystallizes rapidly. Put in bowl or plate and let cool a bit before eating.

WAKAME

A seaweed condiment for rice or other grains.

¶ ¼ cup dried wakame, cut in ½-inch lengths
¶ 2 tablespoons onion flakes
¶ ½ cup water
¶ 1 teaspoon oil

Soak wakame and onion in water for 15 minutes. Strain and reserve liquid. Put oil in bottom of frying pan; add seaweed and onions to pan and stir fry for a few minutes. Add broth and bring to a boil. Reduce heat and cook 5 to 10 minutes.

GARNISHES: ¾ teaspoon lemon juice; ¾ teaspoon tamari soy sauce; stir in ¾ teaspoon miso paste.

TOASTED NORI

These paper-thin sheets of seaweed may be lightly toasted over an open flame. Simply run quickly through fire until color changes and they get crispy. Break in small pieces as a garnish for soups and grains or eat plain. Very nourishing.

VARIATION: rub with sesame oil before toasting.

HOME-DRIED MUSHROOMS

Wash one or more pounds mushrooms and gently wipe dry. String with a needle and heavy thread, with the needle going through the center from top to bottom. Hang horizontally until dry, about 3 days. If you are using large wild mushrooms, slice about ½ inch thick, string as above, putting the needle through sideways, and dry the same way.

GARLIC SPREAD

¶ approximately ⅓ cup

This spread may be made in camp and is good on bread with spaghetti, chili, or just alone when you get a garlic craving.

¶ 12 to 15 large garlic cloves, chopped large
¶ ⅓ cup water
¶ 1 tablespoon butter or olive oil

Combine water and garlic and bring to a boil. Put on low fire and simmer for 10 to 15 minutes or until garlic is done. Add butter or oil and stir well.

SESAME SALT

¶ approximately 1 cup

Known as "gomasio" to some, this wonderful garnish not only heightens flavor, but also adds the valuable food energy of the sesame seed. In a short time you will find yourself sprinkling it on everything you ever used just plain salt on.

¶   1¼ cup sesame seeds, unhulled
¶   ⅛ cup sea salt (or to taste)

Roast sesame seeds, combine with salt. Grind in suribachi, with mortar and pestle, or even a blender. Store in airtight container.

HONEY SYRUP

¶ approximately 1 cup

This can be made at home or in camp. It's very simple to make and warmed up before serving really makes pancakes seem luxurious.

¶   1 cup honey
¶   1 teaspoon vanilla
¶   1 tablespoon water

Warm honey, add water and vanilla; stir well. Heat until honey is syrupy. If you make it at home, you might like to put this in a squeeze bottle and carry ready to pour. Reheat in camp if you like, by submerging bottle in hot water while pancakes cook. (We have used recycled biodegradable soap bottles.) If you have found any fresh berries, you might like to put the syrup in a pan and stir them in.

EMPTYING

Birds swoop down in dance
scattering

> *all thoughts*
> *once caught*
> *dispersed in a moment's time*

a surprise of surprises
that pry the closed womb

> *or Forget-me-nots*
> *answering*
> *subtleties of lavender*

>> *that majestic mountains*
>> *cannot compare*

How closer I become
hovering upon
clumps of green, glistening
in sun

> *or ferns so dearly dressed*
> *in rain, the moist sweet*
> *lips of love*

> *wings of butterflies*
> *from which to drink*

discloses myself to myself
circling with the hawks above.

Laura Kwong

NATURAL REMEDIES

MOUNTAIN PENNYROYAL

A general introduction to natural
health aids.

This section is not meant to
replace any standard first aid or
medical manual,* but to add to it.
So many minor ailments and
discomforts that come up every
now and then can be easily soothed
by things you might be carrying in
your pack: herbs, natural oils,
vitamins, honey, garlic, lemons,
dried fruit.

*See "Books to Read and Use" for a good one.

If any infection or ailment gets out of hand, or looks like it might, get to a lower elevation as soon as possible—as all problems will be worse at higher altitudes—and contact a physician. Some problems may even disappear at lower altitudes. Remember, too, not to get too cold, tired, sweaty or over-extended on a hike.

Take it easy, climb slowly. The air is thinner at higher altitudes, making it easier to get sunburned. Drink a lot of water and use more salt to prevent dehydration.

Take care.

TEAS AnD POULTICES

Finding yourself along the trail or arriving in camp with an unexpected ache or pain can be very unpleasant unless you stay on top of the situation and use a little common sense. Usually water, soap, salt, honey, and the right foods will take care of minor complaints. We list below a few herb teas. The wonderful benefit of these teas is that they may be taken at any time, as they have a "toning" effect on the body. So if you invest in a small amount of herbs to take along for specific reasons, and no one gets hurt or sick, you will still have many delicious cups of tea at hand that your system will appreciate. Herbs keep very well—for at least a year, and some of them several years, if packaged airtight—and are lightweight to pack in. For general information about herb teas, please see the Beverage section, Herbal Tonic Teas.

cayenne, powdered
chamomile blossoms
chickweed leaves
comfrey, root and leaves
flaxseed
ginger, powdered
ginseng, powdered
golden seal, powdered
juniper berries

parsley leaves
pennyroyal leaves
peppermint leaves
plantain leaves
sage leaves
scullcap leaves and
  stems
squaw tea (stems)

HOW TO MAKE A POULTICE: To make a poultice, use either fresh or dried ground herbs. Wash the affected area and apply either fresh herbs which have been bruised or crushed in some way (either between your hands, with a rock, or by chewing them a little), and thereby moistened in their own juices, or dried herbs you have brought along. If the dried herbs are not powdery, try to get them as much so as possible by crushing with the fingertips, rubbing between flat rocks, or pulverizing in a cup with a wooden spoon. Add enough water to make a paste that is not runny, mixing well. Cover with a dressing of a plastic nature to hold the moisture of the herb directly on the affected area for several hours, or as directed below.

BLEEDING: from *minor* cuts, wounds. Wash wound well with water to which you have added a few drops of liquid soap, or with a mild normal salt solution: 1 level teaspoon salt to 1 cup (8 ounces) water. (If you add too much salt, it will sting.) You may sprinkle on powdered cayenne to stop bleeding. A cool poultice of comfrey or plantain may be applied. Cover afflicted area with sterile, or as clean as possible, cloth or dressing and apply light pressure. Make a tea of comfrey, plantain, or cayenne and drink right away. If bleeding is excessive or if there are any signs of complications, be sure to get to a doctor right away.

BLISTERS: Don't open. If the blister should break open, immediately wash well with soap and water, let dry, apply wheat germ oil or vitamin E cream, or even olive oil, if that's all you have. Cover with a bandaid until healed, applying fresh oil and changing bandage as needed. Plantain, comfrey, or golden seal may be used also as a poultice. For blistered feet, we recommend "moleskins." Dr. Scholl's Moleskin can be found in any drugstore. Cut a hole in the center of a square of moleskin about ½ inch bigger than blister. Press on foot, cover with sock, and keep clean. After blister opens, apply an oil mentioned above if possible.

BRUISES: For bad bruises, make a poultice of comfrey, pennyroyal or cayenne and while still warm, put directly on bruise. Cover and let sit 5 minutes or so. Remove, apply fresh poultice and cover with dressing. Leave overnight. Repeat if necessary. You may, instead, gently rub on wheat germ oil from time to time.

BURNS (minor): A burn is an open wound, and should be treated as such. Immediately immerse in cold water, and leave there for 5 minutes or so. Remove from water and, in order to clean any possible dirt out, pour soap and water or a salt water solution over the burn. (Avoid bothering the area as much as possible.) Carefully pat dry and air briefly. A cool or body-temperature healing poultice of powdered golden seal, comfrey, or plantain may be applied, or cover area with honey or olive or wheat germ oil. Apply a clean fluffy dressing or cloth (Ace bandage preferably) and cover with compression on wound to keep fluid in, as loss of fluid through a large burn is often a danger. Keep covered for 3 days before changing, if possible.

CHAPPED SKIN, SUNBURN, WINDBURN: Rub in wheat germ, olive, apricot, or almond oil. In the case of sunburn, swim in cold water or apply cold wet cloth. Stay in the shade. Re-apply oils as often as your body soaks them up.

CUTS AND SCRAPES: Wash well, soak in salt water. Keep clean and free of infection. Apply wheat germ oil or vitamin E cream or oil. A tea or poultice may be made of comfrey, plantain, golden seal, or chamomile. Either bathe area with tea or cover with a body-temperature poultice. Keep soft with oil.

EYEBURN FROM GLARE, SNOW AND SUN: Make a tea of chamomile or chickweed. Soak cloth in cool tea. Lay wet cloth over closed eyes, being sure that a few drops get into them to rinse them somewhat. Repeat 3 times.

FATIGUE: Most fatigue is heat intoxication (a major loss of fluids and salt, causing a state of dizziness, lightheadedness, and even shock. It is not to be confused with heat stroke, in which the afflicted person gets red in the face, has a very high fever, and loses as much as ¼ of his body weight.): take extra salt, drink *lots* of water to which honey has been added, if possible. Try to sleep or just rest. Breathe freely, follow your breath, and make sure you breathe. Don't over-eat, keep bowels loose, and drink hot tea of ginseng, cayenne or peppermint. (See Hypothermia.)

HEADACHE: Drink lots of water. Note whether the problem stems from heat, fatigue, nerves or eye-strain and, if so, follow their particular remedies. Headaches are often also caused by constipation. If you are sure this is the case, drink lots of water; eat "purgative" fruits and drink their juices; drink 4 to 5 cups a day of tea made of chickweed, ginger, peppermint, or cayenne. If the problem persists, or is serious, or might be a sign of another problem, be sure to see a doctor.

INFECTIONS, SKIN (minor):   Make a poultice of dried ground plantain or comfrey and warm water, cover infection, and put on a bandaid. If no herbs are available, make a compress with warm salt water (1 level teaspoon salt per cup of water) and apply. Change poultice every couple hours or so, or if just using salt water, soak area 4 to 6 times a day, trying to bring infection to a "head." If possible, drink tea of golden seal powder (1 cup 3 times a day) or take it in capsules (1 "00" capsule 3 times a day). When it comes to a "head," sterilize knife (everyone should have a good sharp knife along) with flame or by boiling or with soap and water; make cut where head is large enough that you don't have to squeeze hard (if you apply too much pressure, you'll break down the wall around infection, and it might travel elsewhere); remove pus and treat as open wound.

MOSQUITO BITES: Warm, sweaty skin attracts mosquitos. Rub on pennyroyal or eucalyptus oil; take vitamin B complex daily. Put lemon juice or vinegar on bites.

MUSCLE PAIN: Remember that a "charley-horse" is a muscle spasm. Treat muscle aches by stretching and using muscles, as the pain is caused by muscle contraction. If you stop using them altogether, muscles will tighten and get sorer. If possible, apply warm compresses of cloth soaked in chamomile or comfrey tea. Re-soak cloth every 15 minutes or so and repeat for 1 hour.

NERVES, CALMATIVES: It's hard to imagine anyone needing one of these teas in the back country, but you never know. Take a cup of warm tea 3 times a day or before going to bed of any one or combination of the following: chamomile, scullcap, golden seal or peppermint. Chew on fresh pennyroyal leaves, if available.

STRESS AND INABILITY TO ADJUST TO ALTITUDE CHANGE: Symptoms: Combination of headache, fever, extreme fatigue, quick shallow breathing, sweating and nausea. First thing to do is to lie down and rest. If the problem isn't solved by resting, go to a lower elevation. Drink lots of water and take diuretic teas—any one of the following: plantain, parsley, juniper berries, chamomile, scullcap, golden seal, or flaxseed.

LACK OF FRESH FOODS: Take extra vitamin C (try to get organic vitamin C) or take vitamin B complex, or a tea of either or both juniper berries and flaxseed. Keep handy, especially on winter trips.

FOOD SHORTAGE: In case food supply is dangerously low, and you need every bit of nutrition you can find, drink comfrey, sage, or squaw tea, or make a weak solution (1 tablespoon per cup) of rice, rye, or oats, and drink as a tea. These are very lightweight, to pack in a bit extra for emergencies.

TOO COLD: Wear wool shirts and sweaters, as wool keeps you warm even when it's wet. We recommend "layering," using cotton and wool clothing. To prevent getting chilled, the minute you start perspiring take off the top layer until you're down to your skin, if you have to be. As soon as you stop working hard, start putting the layers back on, slowly, to retain the body heat that you've built up from working and sweating. If you get chilled before you put your clothes back on, it's very hard to get warm again. We have found that carrying the little extra weight of wool clothing will pay off. Keep your hat on, you lose a lot of heat through the top of your head.

HYPOTHERMIA: Is as acute as heat stroke, only in the opposite direction. Hypothermia means basically that a person is cold clear to the bone, and that all of his body's defensive resources are nearly exhausted. If he gets any colder, he will die. When in this state, he no longer has the ability to realize that he is cold. It could happen under any particular set of circumstances—after a rainstorm or a fall in a lake, or whatever, and is a critical condition that should be treated on the trail, if necessary. The individual should be warmed up and fed immediately, wrapped in a bedroll, put by a warm fire, and given warm, nutritional teas with honey.

WINTER TEA TO WARM YOU UP: a stimulating, energizing tea is a combination of: ginseng, cayenne, ginger and juniper berries. Serve with lemon juice and drink hot.

TOO HOT: Drink a lot of liquids, and take extra salt. Wear cotton clothing, as its natural fibers breathe better than those of nylon and other synthetics. Wear a light-colored straw or cotton hat. For an exhilarating treat, dip the top of your head in a stream and let the cool water run down your face when you stand up. Sometimes it feels good and helps to soak a bandana handkerchief in a stream and wrap it loosely around your neck. Try washing your hands and arms to the elbows with water; even soaking your feet for a few minutes will help. Ben Kinmont likes to soak his hat in a creek, fill it with water and dump it on top of his head as he puts his hat on. (See Fatigue.)

SUMMER TEA TO COOL YOU DOWN: This tea could be started early in the morning, put in the sun and left in a creek just before lunch, or in the early afternoon. In the heat of the day when you are tired of frolicking, sit in the shade and drink. Or the tea could be made in the morning and carried along on hikes until it is cooler and the sun is hotter. Use chickweed, plantain and/or peppermint. Serve with lemon juice, if you have some. Drink lots.

3.

Appendices

MENUS

Here are 2 menu plans: one for an extensive 10-day trip like the one described in the Foreword, and one for the usual weekend or 3-day trip.

The 10-day menu is planned with higher protein meals toward the end when you will need the protein the most, after using a lot of energy.

The 3-day menu includes more fresh foods and weight per day, since it's easier to carry relatively heavier loads per day on short trips.

Cook extra pancakes for breakfast and save leftovers for lunch. Plan some drinks ahead of time so they will be ready when you return from a hike.

The foods used here are all long-lasting, with the exception of the fresh fruits, vegetables, and cheeses. The fresh foods will usually last up to a week. To preserve cheese awhile longer for extensive trips or for food caches, wrap in cheesecloth, dip in melted wax, and let set. Butter will last for a couple of weeks if carried in a plastic container and stored in the shade.

10-DAY MENU FOR TWO

BREAKFAST SUGGESTIONS

Mountain Gruel Cereal
raisins, honey, butter
rose hip, mint tea

Buckwheat Pancakes
honey, syrup, butter
fresh yarrow, red clover tea or
raspberry leaf, wintergreen tea with lemon

Cold Morning Wheat Cereal
dates, walnuts
Hot Carob Milk

Brown Rice Flour Pancakes
maple syrup, butter
sassafras, sarsparilla tea with honey

Stewed Fruit over Granola or with
Hot Chapatis and peanut butter
mint tea

Soaked Cereal with Cashew Milk
Hot Carob Milk

Whole Wheat Soy Pancakes
maple syrup, peanut butter
alfalfa, rose hip, mint tea with lemon

Wheat Germ Cereal with
Seed Cereal Topping
fresh pennyroyal tea

Stewed Fruit

Mountain Gruel Cereal
powdered milk, wheat germ, dates, honey

and the long walk out.

LUNCH SUGGESTIONS

High Protein Crackers
Polenta Cakes
Soybean Cakes
leftover pancakes
cheese
Miso Sesame Butter Spread
peanut butter
dry hot mustard
dried fruit
nuts
Popped Seeds or Toasted Soybeans
Peanut Butter Fudge, 1 pound
Seed Date Fudge, ½ pound
oranges
lemons for Lemonade
Five-Grain Soup
High Protein Almond Cookies
Fruit Leather

Eggplant Parmesan
Creamy Tapioca Pudding
catnip tea

Plain Brown Rice with soy sauce
hot vegetable broth

Miso Soup

Seafood Curry over wheat-soy noodles
whole wheat chapatis, butter
mint tea

Corn Bean Mush with cheese
6 High Protein Crackers
alfalfa, mint, lemon grass tea

Spinach Cheese Soup
popcorn
Rose Hip Drink

Sesame Seed Patties with
Mushroom Gravy
Apple Crisp
mint tea

Garlic Broth with
Fish Dumplings *or*
noodles and wild greens
Polenta Cakes
yarrow, red clover tea

Chili with cheese
Cornbread and butter
raspberry leaf, mint, comfrey tea

Miso Soup with buckwheat noodles and mountain
sorrel
High Mountain Pie
pennyroyal tea

3-DAY MENU FOR TWO

BREAKFAST SUGGESTIONS

Hot Cracked Millet Cream Cereal with
black walnuts, dates, and coconut
Rose Hip Drink

Corn Pancakes with
peanut butter and/or maple syrup
peppermint, chamomile tea

Bulgar Corn Meal Cereal with
Topping
Hot Carob Drink

LUNCH SUGGESTIONS

Sesame Seed Crackers with
Bongko Bean Spread
cheese
dried figs
Lemonade

Potato Cakes with hot mustard
Salad of fresh greens *or* 1 sliced cucumber with
Miso Salad Dressing
peppermint, chamomile tea cold (make extra at
breakfast)

cheese
all the good leftovers
fresh cold water

Polenta Cheese Soup
Meal Cakes with
Date Walnut Topping
red clover, comfrey tea with lemon

Spaghetti with
Tomato Sauce
Cheese Toasties made with leftover pancakes
catnip tea with honey

Fish Patties with lemon
Tomato Noodle Soup
fresh yarrow tea

EXTRAS

dried fruit
nuts
Pecan Fudge
Sesame Seed Cookies
sunflower seeds, raisins
fruit juice concentrate

"The man who sat on the ground in his tipi meditating on life and its meaning, accepting the kinship of all creatures and acknowledging unity with the universe of things was infusing into his being the true essence of civilization. And when native man left off this form of development, his humanization was retarded in growth."

–Chief Luther Standing Bear

CARING FOR THE BACK COUNTRY

- ¶ Carry out all plastic, tin cans, aluminum foil, and paper. Don't leave anything behind but footprints.
- ¶ Discard cold dishwater and small organic leftovers under a bush or tree—not in the water, as any food or animal products will sink to the bottom, rot, and pollute. Carry out or bury orange or lemon peels and other things that take a long time to return to the earth.
- ¶ Use only biodegradable soap, such as liquid castile.
- ¶ Use white toilet paper instead of colored, as the dyes won't biodegrade. Dig a deep hole and bury it, but please not near the water or trail.
- ¶ Use a stove. If you absolutely must have a fire, use existing fireplaces, and clean them up afterwards.
- ¶ Leave wrappers in your pocket, not on the trail.

WHERE TO BUY FOOD

Your own favorite natural food store, grocery, and supermarket. Chinese and Japanese food stores. We are familiar with:

Uoki K. Sakai, Co.
1656 Post Street
San Francisco, California 94115

For those on the West Coast, there are also several good shops on Grant and Post streets in Chinatown and Japantown, in San Francisco.

Suppliers of bulk dehydrated and freeze-dried foods:

Ken's Mountaineering and Backpacking
155 North Edison Way
Reno, Nevada 89502

The Smilie Company
575 Howard Street
San Francisco, California 94105

(Write for mail-order forms and price lists.)

BOOKS TO READ AND USE

BACK TO EDEN, by Jethro Kloss, Longview Publishing House, Coalmont, Tennessee, 1970

DIET FOR A SMALL PLANET, by Frances Moore Lappe, Friends of the Earth/Ballantine Books, New York, 1971

KINSHIP WITH ALL LIFE, by J. Allen Boone, Harper and Row, New York, 1954

LETTERS OF A WOMAN HOMESTEADER, by Elinore Pruitt Stewart, Bison Books, University of Nebraska Press, Lincoln, Nebraska, 1967

LIGHTWEIGHT BACKPACKING, by Charles L. Jansen, Bantam Books, New York, 1974

MEDICINE FOR MOUNTAINEERING, edited by James A. Wilkerson. The Mountaineers, Seattle, Washington, 1967

MOUNTAINEERING MEDICINE, by Fred T. Darvill, Jr., M.D., Skagit Mountain Rescue Unit, Inc., P.O. Box 2, Mt. Vernon, Washington, 98273

SEVEN ARROWS, by Hyemeyohsts Storm, Harper and Row, New York, 1972

TASSAJARA COOKING, by Edward Espe Brown, Shambala Press, Berkeley, California, 1973

TEN TALENTS, by Frank and Rosalie Hurd, Box 86-A, Route 1, Chisolm, Minnesota, 55719, 1968 (available by mail order)

THE CROSS-COUNTRY SKI COOK LOOK AND PLEASURE BOOK AND WELCOME TO THE ALICE IN SNOWPEOPLE LAND, by Hal Painter, Wilderness Press, Berkeley, California, 1974

THE SECRET LIFE OF PLANTS, by Peter Tompkins and Christopher Bird, Avon Books, New York, 1973

WILD EDIBLE PLANTS OF THE WESTERN UNITED STATES, by Donald Kirk, Naturegraph Publishers, Healdsburg, California, 1970

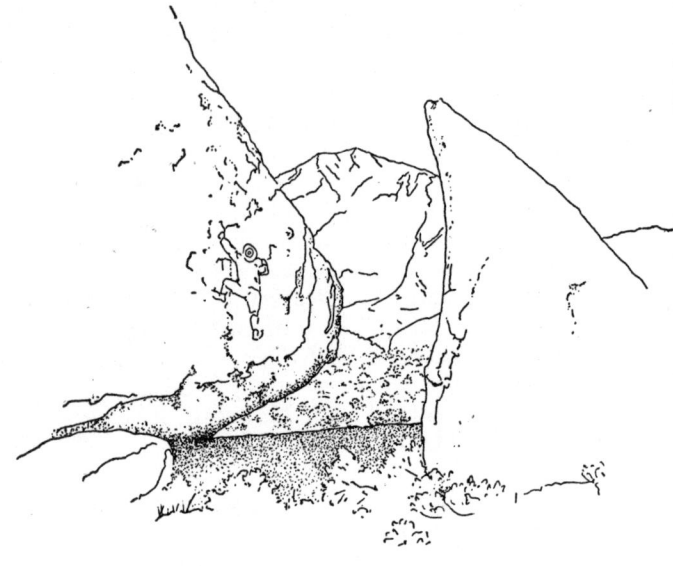

With all that evolving spread out behind us
We dance this frost fall morning away
On the sunward sides
Of granite boulders

–Doug Robinson

INDEX

ACKNOWLEDGMENTS

Together we thank: Bob for the illustrations, Doug for his writings, Dr. Bob Denton and Dr. John Christopher for help on the Natural Remedies section, and Laura for her poem.

And for support, encouragement and enthusiasm, individually,

Claudia thanks: Louie Bergeron; Tom Burke; Marlene Miller; Richard Ashcroft; Dick Barrubi; and Brad Smith.

and Vikki thanks: Ben, Anna and Seth Kinmont, my children; Bill and Laura Kwong; Sue Allan; Tom and Amy Valens; Susan Jensen; Livia Davis; Jan Mason; and Red Valens.

And we both thank all the people who have helped us separately to recognize the path which is ours.

NOTES

NOTES

NOTES

NOTES

NOTES

NOTES

NOTES

NOTES

NOTES

NOTES